SPIRITUAL WARFARE

Living in the Victory of Christ

ROBERT GRIFFITH

GRACE AND TRUTH PUBLISHING
P.O. Box 338, Gunnedah NSW 2380 Australia
www.graceandtruthpublishing.com.au

ISBN 978-1-7642635-3-5

TABLE OF CONTENTS

PREFACE

Spiritual warfare is not a side topic for the spiritually elite. It is the daily reality of every single Christian. Whether we recognise it or not, we are engaged in a battle that is unseen, but very real. It touches our minds, our relationships, our decisions, and our sense of identity in Christ.

In many years of pastoral ministry, I've witnessed two extremes that often hinder believers. One is denial — treating Satan and his schemes as totally irrelevant in the modern world. The other is obsession — attributing every hardship to demonic activity and living in fear. Both distort the truth and disarm God's people.

This book is written to provide a thorough, biblical and balanced understanding of spiritual warfare. It's not a manual for experts or a collection of dramatic stories. It's a call to wake up — not with panic, but with clarity. To recognise the battle for what it is. To understand our enemy, our authority in Christ, and the spiritual weapons which are at our disposal.

Each chapter concludes with the question: *'How then shall I live?'* Because this is not just a topic to explore - it is a life to live. A life of resistance and rest. A life of discernment and peace and Spirit-empowered confidence rooted in the finished work of Jesus.

If you feel overwhelmed, confused, or ill-equipped, take heart. You are not alone. You are not without help. And you are not without hope. Always remember, the One who is in you, is greater than the one who is in the world.

Let's stand firm — together.

Robert Griffith

1. THE UNSEEN BATTLE: UNDERSTANDING THE REALITY OF SPIRITUAL WARFARE

A battle we cannot see

The Christian life is not a playground — it is a battleground. From the moment we enter into relationship with Christ, we are caught up in a conflict that transcends the physical and touches the eternal. This conflict is not one we can see with our natural eyes. It is not fought with guns or politics or persuasive arguments.

It is a spiritual battle, fought in the unseen realm, with very real consequences that ripple through every area of our lives. To ignore this reality is to live in illusion. To obsess over it is to be paralyzed by fear. To understand it rightly is to walk in victory, equipped and confident in the One who has already triumphed.

Paul wrote to the church in Ephesus, saying, *"Finally, be strong in the Lord and in his mighty power. Put on the full armour of God, so that you can take your stand against the devil's schemes. For our struggle is not against flesh and blood, but against the rulers, against the authorities, against the powers of this dark world and against the spiritual forces of evil in the heavenly realms."* (Ephesians 6:10–12). That brief passage is packed with vital truth: there is a struggle; it is personal; it is spiritual; and it is real. Yet many Christians today live as though none of that is true.

For some, the entire idea of spiritual warfare seems archaic or superstitious — perhaps even a bit embarrassing. In an age that prizes rationalism and science, talk of devils and demons feels more at home in medieval folklore than modern theology. But Scripture does not apologise for the unseen world. It assumes its reality on nearly every page. From Genesis to Revelation, we find angels and demons, battles and temptations, victories and defeats — all pointing to a conflict beyond what we can touch or measure normally. Jesus Himself constantly acknowledged and confronted this invisible war. He cast out demons, He rebuked Satan, and He taught His disciples to pray for deliverance from the evil one.

To follow Jesus, then, is to take very seriously the reality He acknowledged and engaged. Yet if one error is to deny the spiritual battle altogether, the opposite error is to be consumed by it. Some believers become fixated on Satan and his works, seeing demonic involvement behind every frustration, sickness, or setback. They live in fear, blaming the devil for everything from car troubles to burnt toast, attributing to him a level of power and presence he simply does not possess. Such an approach not only distorts biblical teaching but also distracts us from our true focus — Jesus Christ. Spiritual warfare is real, yes, but it is not the central theme of the Christian life. Christ is. And in Him, we are more than conquerors.

The cosmic conflict behind our story

Understanding spiritual warfare begins when we recognise the broader context of Scripture: there is a cosmic conflict between the Kingdom of God and the kingdom of darkness. This conflict did not begin on earth but in heaven, when Lucifer, a created angel, rebelled against his Creator and sought to usurp His throne. That rebellion marked the origin of spiritual warfare, and it continues to unfold until the final consummation of God's purposes in Jesus Christ. In this cosmic narrative, we are not spectators — we are participants. Our lives matter. Our choices count. Our prayers, obedience, and faith all have weight in this unseen struggle. We are not victims caught in the crossfire; we are soldiers enlisted in a cause far greater than ourselves.

But we must understand the nature of this battle. Paul said our struggle is not against flesh and blood. That is a very radical statement. It means that ultimately, people are not our enemies. Not governments, not cultural movements, not even those who oppose us most violently. Behind every visible conflict lies an invisible influence.

This does not mean every hardship or every disagreement has a demonic cause, but it does mean that we must learn to look beyond the surface. The true enemy of the church is not any political figure or social trend — it is the adversary of our souls who seeks to steal, kill, and destroy.

Satan is a deceiver. His primary weapon is the lie. Jesus called him the *"father of lies"* and said, *"When he lies, he speaks his native language."* (John 8:44). From the Garden of Eden. Right through to the temptation of Christ in the wilderness, the enemy has always used deception as his first line of attack. He twists truth, sows doubt and tempts with promises he cannot fulfil. He does not usually appear in grotesque form or announce his presence. He whispers, questions, and manipulates. His lies are wrapped in partial truths, appealing to our desires and fears. That is why discernment is so critical. To stand firm in spiritual warfare is not about shouting louder prayers or casting out demons at every turn — it is about knowing the truth and standing in it.

The armour of daily dependence

This is why Paul urges believers to *"put on the full armour of God."* Each piece of that armour is rooted in truth, righteousness, peace, faith, salvation, and the Word of God. These are not magical tools but spiritual realities, grounded in our relationship with Christ. The armour is not something we put on once and forget — it is a daily posture, a way of life. To wear the belt of truth is to refuse the lies of the enemy. To wear the breastplate of righteousness is to walk in the righteousness of Christ, not our own. To carry the shield of faith is to trust God's promises when everything else says otherwise. This is how we stand — not in our strength, but in His. The armour of God is only an analogy. All the pieces of this armour represent Christ. When we have Christ, we already have the armour we need. By saying *"put on"* the armour of God, Paul is simply saying, *"Use what you have been given in Christ!"*

The battlefield is not always dramatic. It is quite often subtle. It happens in the quiet corners of our minds and hearts, in the choices we make when no one is watching, in the thoughts we entertain and the narratives we believe. Spiritual warfare is not reserved for exorcisms or crises — it is woven into the fabric of our daily discipleship. The decision to forgive when bitterness beckons is warfare. The refusal to gossip when the opportunity arises is warfare. The discipline to pray when we feel dry and distracted is warfare.

In every moment, we are either advancing the Kingdom or retreating before the enemy's schemes. There is a sobering reality here, but also a liberating one. If spiritual warfare is constant and unseen, it means we must be alert—but not afraid. Scripture never calls us to fear the devil. Quite the opposite. We are told to resist him, and he will flee. We are reminded that the One who is in us is greater than the one who is in the world. We are assured that Christ has already disarmed the powers and authorities, triumphing over them by the cross. The victory is not in doubt. The war is won. But the battle still rages as the enemy seeks to destroy as much as he can before his final defeat.

Spiritual warfare for us is actually not about gaining victory; it is about enforcing the victory Christ has already secured. It is like the cleanup after a decisive battle has been won. The enemy has been mortally wounded, but he fights on, desperate and furious, seeking to inflict maximum damage. He cannot reclaim what Christ has redeemed, but he can certainly sow confusion, fear, and division if we allow him to. That is why we must remain vigilant. Not anxious. Not paranoid. But alert, rooted, and ready.

This posture is not passive. To be a Christian is to be engaged in the resistance. But our weapons are not of this world. As Paul wrote in 2 Corinthians 10:4, *"The weapons we fight with are not the weapons of the world. On the contrary, they have divine power to demolish strongholds."* Strongholds are not just those demonic presences—they are patterns of thought, entrenched lies, and systems of rebellion that exalt themselves against the knowledge of God. Our battle is not simply to survive, but to tear down these strongholds through truth, prayer, and obedience.

One of the greatest strongholds in our modern age is apathy. The enemy would rather have a church that is asleep than one that is outright hostile. If he can lull us into complacency, convince us that all is well, and distract us with trivial pursuits, he has effectively neutralized our witness. Spiritual warfare today often looks like choosing depth over distraction, truth over trend, and faithfulness over fame. It is the slow, steady, costly obedience to Christ in a world that constantly pulls us in another direction.

Another great danger is fear. When we give Satan more credit than he deserves, when we speak more about his power than Christ's, we empower a defeated foe. Fear gives ground to the enemy. It makes us shrink back when we should stand firm. It makes us question what God has already spoken. That is why Scripture is filled with the command, *"Do not be afraid."* Not because there is nothing fearful in the world, but because our God is greater than anything we face. The antidote to fear is not denial — it is faith. It is trust in the character of God and the sufficiency of His Word.

This unseen battle touches every part of our lives — our minds, our relationships, our churches, our culture. It is not limited to moments of crisis or overt evil. It is present in the decisions we make, the beliefs we hold, and the voices we listen to. And yet, we are not called to obsess over the enemy or chase every shadow. We are called to fix our eyes on Jesus, the author and perfecter of our faith. He is our victory, our strength, and our security.

The more we understand the spiritual battle, the more we see the necessity of abiding in Christ. He is the vine — we are the branches. Cut off from Him, we can do nothing. But in Him, we bear fruit, resist evil, and walk in peace. The Christian life is not about trying harder — it is about trusting deeper. Spiritual warfare is not won by sheer effort, but by deep dependence on the One who has already overcome.

Spiritual warfare in the lives of God's people

The presence of spiritual warfare in the biblical narrative is not incidental — it is pervasive. It appears not only in moments of dramatic confrontation but also in the ordinary stories of faith, failure, and redemption that shape the lives of God's people. From Adam and Eve's first temptation in Eden to the final defeat of Satan in the book of Revelation, the Bible tells the story of a cosmic struggle played out in real human lives. But it also makes clear that the outcome of this war is not in doubt. The decisive victory belongs to God, and His people are called not to win the battle anew, but to live faithfully in light of that victory.

Take, for instance, the story of Job. Behind the visible suffering of this righteous man was a spiritual dimension unknown to Job himself. Satan appears before God, accusing Job of serving Him only because of the blessings he enjoys. With God's permission, Satan is allowed to test Job—but with strict limitations. What unfolds is a profound testimony to the nature of faith in suffering, but also a powerful reminder that our lives are often the stage upon which unseen spiritual realities are contested. Job never knew the full extent of what had taken place behind the curtain of his affliction. And yet, his perseverance testified to the glory of God and silenced the accuser.

In the New Testament, we see the same dynamic in the life of Peter. In Luke 22:31–32, on the night Jesus was betrayed, He turned to His disciple and said, *"Simon, Simon, Satan has asked to sift all of you as wheat. But I have prayed for you, Simon, that your faith may not fail."* Notice that Jesus does not prevent the test, but He intercedes for Peter's faith. The battle is spiritual. The weapon is prayer. The goal is endurance. Peter's eventual restoration and leadership in the early church become a powerful witness to the truth that while the enemy may test us, God uses even those trials to refine and strengthen us.

Paul's ministry is also marked by an acute awareness of the spiritual battle. In his letters, he regularly warns of false teachers, demonic influence, and spiritual deception. He describes Satan as masquerading as *"an angel of light"* and warns that his servants often appear as servants of righteousness. In 2 Corinthians 10:3, Paul reminds the church that though we live in the world, *"we do not wage war as the world does."* Instead, we demolish arguments and every pretension that sets itself up against the knowledge of God. This is not a battle fought with violence or manipulation— it is a battle for the mind, for truth, and for hearts surrendered to Jesus Christ.

This understanding of spiritual warfare is crucial. It reminds us that not all threats are visible. The most dangerous attacks on the church are not always external persecution but often internal compromise.

The enemy rarely launches a frontal assault when a subtle whisper will do. He infiltrates through pride, division, legalism, false teaching, and distraction. He loves when Christians fight each other instead of fighting him. He rejoices when churches lose sight of the gospel and then become consumed with performance, politics, or personality cults. Spiritual warfare is not always spectacular — it is often subtle. But its effects are devastating when left unchallenged.

The weapons of truth, prayer, and community

One of the greatest battlegrounds in spiritual warfare is the human mind. Paul urges believers in Romans 12:2, *"Do not conform to the pattern of this world, but be transformed by the renewing of your mind."* The enemy's lies often begin with subtle distortions — questions like *"Did God really say ..?"* or suggestions that we are unloved, unworthy, or unforgivable. These lies, if left unchecked, become strongholds — patterns of thought that shape our identity and behaviour.

The renewing of the mind through Scripture, prayer, and the work of the Holy Spirit is not a luxury — it is a necessity. Truth must take the place of lies if we are to live in freedom.

Jesus' own confrontation with Satan in the wilderness is a model of spiritual warfare. After fasting for forty days, He is tempted by the devil with three direct challenges — each appealing to physical need, pride, and power. But Jesus does not argue or negotiate. He responds with Scripture. *"It is written..."* is His constant reply. This is not mere quotation — it is warfare. Jesus wields the Word of God as a sword, countering each temptation with truth. In doing so, He shows us how to stand. Victory does not come from cleverness, intensity, or emotion. It comes from truth rightly applied in the moment of testing.

The authority of Scripture is central in spiritual warfare. In a world saturated with opinions, ideologies, and conflicting messages, the Word of God is our unshakable foundation. It reveals the nature of God, the schemes of the enemy, and the promises we can cling to when the battle rages.

To neglect the Word is to fight blindfolded and unarmed. To know it, meditate on it, and live by it is to be equipped for every assault. This is not a call to the legalistic study of the Bible, it is a call to immersive, transformative engagement with the living Word. It is how we learn to recognize the enemy's voice—and more importantly, how we learn to recognize God's.

Prayer is another critical weapon in spiritual warfare. Not as a ritual or obligation, but as communion with God Himself and participation in His purposes. In Ephesians 6, after describing the armour of God, Paul writes, *"And pray in the Spirit on all occasions with all kinds of prayers and requests."* Prayer is not just preparation for the battle—it is the battle. It aligns our hearts with God's will, strengthens our resolve, and invites divine intervention into our earthly situations. Daniel's experience in chapter 10 of his book is striking—he prays for 21 days before receiving an answer, and when the angel arrives, he explains that he was delayed by spiritual resistance. This mysterious glimpse reminds us that prayer engages realities beyond our perception. It matters more than we know.

But prayer is not just defensive—it is also offensive. It tears down strongholds, releases captives, and advances God's Kingdom. When the early church prayed, prison doors opened, boldness increased, and the gospel spread fast. When Jesus taught His disciples to pray, He included the words, *"Deliver us from the evil one."* That is not some kind of passive hope—it is a declaration of dependence and a cry for victory. Prayer is how we resist the devil. It is how we remain watchful. It is how we invite the power of God into the daily realities of temptation, oppression, and spiritual pressure.

Community also plays a vital role in spiritual warfare. The Christian life was never meant to be lived in isolation. We are members of a body, soldiers in an army, and stones in a living temple. The enemy loves to isolate believers, to convince them they are alone, misunderstood, or too broken to belong. But when we gather, pray, confess, worship, and bear one another's burdens, we create a spiritual environment where the enemy cannot thrive.

Light exposes darkness. Truth dismantles lies. Unity silences accusation. This is why division in the church is so deadly—it severs our strength and compromises our witness.

Hebrews 10:24-25 reminds us not to give up meeting together, but to encourage one another—and all the more as we see the Day approaching. Spiritual warfare increases as the return of Christ draws near. The enemy knows his time is short. But so do we. And that knowledge should lead not to panic, but to purpose. We are not called to hide or retreat, but to stand firm, linked arm in arm with our brothers and sisters, declaring by our unity and love that the gates of hell shall not prevail.

The power of worship and obedience

Worship is another great weapon, often overlooked but deeply powerful. When we worship, we declare the truth of who God is in the face of every lie. We lift our eyes from the battle to the Victor. We align our hearts with heaven. Worship silences the accuser, strengthens our faith, and reminds us of our eternal perspective. Paul and Silas, imprisoned and beaten, sang hymns in the night—and God shook the foundations of the prison. Worship is not escapism—it is engagement. It is choosing to praise in the middle of the storm, to believe in the dark what God has shown in the light.

Many years ago, I was instrumental in launching and running a city-wide worship event called *'Sunday Night Live.'* We ran between 8 and 10 of these events each year and had people from all the Churches in our town involved. There was no teaching or preaching - just 90 minutes of worship and prayer in the largest venue in our town.

Over the years we ran these worship evenings, there were literally hundreds of testimonies of demonic strongholds being demolished across our community. People were being healed. Marriages were repaired. Even the local economy was thriving during that time. I have no doubt this all flowed from the city-wide worship which had never happened before.

There is also profound spiritual power in obedience. Sometimes we look for dramatic spiritual experiences, forgetting that the most potent form of spiritual warfare is often quiet, consistent faithfulness. Every time we choose truth over lies, purity over compromise, generosity over greed, or humility over pride, we are participating in spiritual resistance. The enemy cannot stand a believer who obeys God even when it costs, even when it's hard. That kind of obedience undermines his authority and magnifies God's glory.

Yet we must be clear: spiritual warfare is not primarily about technique or intensity — it is about relationship. We do not fight *for* victory; we fight *from* victory. Our authority comes not from volume, experience, or ritual, but from our union with Christ. In Him, we are seated in heavenly places. In Him, we are more than conquerors. In Him, the enemy has no rightful claim. But apart from Him, we are powerless.

The seven sons of Sceva learned this the hard way in Acts 19. Attempting to cast out demons *"in the name of Jesus whom Paul preaches,"* they were attacked and humiliated. The demons did not recognize their authority — because they had none. They knew Paul. They knew Jesus. But the imitators had no spiritual weight.

This story is a warning against superficial engagement with deep realities. Spiritual warfare is not a game. It is not about formulas or bravado. It is about being rooted in Christ, filled with the Spirit, and walking in obedience. It is all about knowing God deeply, loving Him truly, and standing firm in His truth. It is about surrender, not swagger.

Many believers feel unequipped for spiritual warfare because they assume it requires special training or dramatic encounters. But Scripture paints a different picture. The primary battlefield is the heart and the mind. The primary weapons are truth, righteousness, faith, the Word, and prayer. The primary calling is to stand — not to chase demons, not to seek signs, but to stand. And in Christ, we are fully equipped to do so.

There will be moments of intense pressure, temptation, and attack. There will be seasons when the enemy seems unusually active, when doubts rise, fears whisper, and circumstances shake. But none of these are signs that God has abandoned us. Quite the opposite. Often, they are the refining fires through which our faith is purified, our witness strengthened, and our dependence deepened. The enemy attacks what he fears. If you feel the weight of spiritual battle, it may be because you are a threat to the kingdom of darkness.

However, even in the battle, there is peace. Peace is not the absence of conflict — it is the presence of Christ in the midst of it. Jesus said, *"Peace I leave with you; my peace I give you. I do not give to you as the world gives. Do not let your hearts be troubled and do not be afraid."* That peace is not fragile — it is fierce. It holds us when the winds rise. It anchors us when the waves crash. It is a peace that surpasses understanding because it is rooted not in circumstances but in the character of God.

This is the spiritual life. Not a sheltered existence but a secured one. Not a life without trouble, but a life filled with presence. In Christ, we are not called to fear the enemy, but to resist him. Not to obsess over evil, but to overcome it with good. Not to fight for ourselves, but to stand in the victory already won by our King.

Scripture teaches us about Satan not to fascinate us, but to equip us. His titles reveal his tactics: he is the accuser, the tempter, the deceiver, the destroyer. He sows lies where God has spoken truth. He tempts us to seek what God has already promised, but on our own terms. He accuses us after we fall, convincing us that grace is not sufficient. He divides churches, distracts saints, and distorts doctrine. But he always does so under God's sovereign leash. He cannot act outside the boundaries God permits. He is certainly not God's equal. He is not omnipresent, omniscient, or omnipotent. He is a created being, fallen and condemned, whose doom is certain. The danger lies in forgetting that. Many believers live with a functional dualism, as if Satan and God are locked in an ongoing tug-of-war, with the outcome in doubt.

This is not biblical. God is sovereign. Christ is King. The Spirit is present. The devil is defeated. That does not make him harmless — it makes him desperate. He still prowls like a roaring lion, seeking whom he may devour. But the roar is not the final word. We are not called to fear the roar — we are called to resist it, firm in the faith.

Our resistance is not rooted in rituals or incantations. It is rooted in knowing the truth and walking in it. James 4:7 tell us, *"Submit yourselves, then, to God. Resist the devil, and he will flee from you."* Note the order: submission to God precedes resistance to the devil. We cannot resist while we are walking in compromise. Authority comes from alignment. When we are submitted to the will and Word of God, we stand on solid ground. The devil flees not because of us, but because of the One in whom we stand.

We must also understand that not every difficulty is demonic. Life in a fallen world includes suffering, disappointment, and human weakness. The flesh is a formidable enemy. So is the world's system of thinking. Not every headache is an attack. Not every temptation is a possession. Wisdom will always require discernment — learning to distinguish between natural trials, fleshly patterns, and genuine spiritual opposition. But regardless of the source, the solution is the same: abiding in Christ, standing in truth, praying in faith, and walking in obedience.

A church prepared for war

The church has a central role in spiritual warfare — not merely as a collection of individual warriors, but as a united body standing against the gates of hell. Jesus promised in Matthew 16 that the gates of Hades would not prevail against His church. That statement is not defensive — it is actually offensive. Gates are not weapons. They are defensive structures. The image is of the church storming the gates, advancing the Kingdom, tearing down strongholds with the gospel of truth and grace. But how often the church has reversed this posture. In fear, we retreat. In apathy, we slumber. In division, we weaken. A church unaware of spiritual warfare becomes vulnerable.

A church obsessed with it becomes unhealthy. But a church grounded in truth, clothed in humility, equipped with the Word, and led by the Spirit—such a church is a force the enemy cannot withstand. Warfare is not just the task of pastors or prayer warriors—it is the calling of every believer. And it happens not only in revivals or deliverance meetings, but also in our staff meetings, family dinners, counselling sessions, mission trips, neighbourhood walks, and everyday conversations. Every time truth is spoken in love, every time forgiveness is chosen over bitterness, every time hope is proclaimed in the face of despair, spiritual ground is claimed. We overcome by the blood of the Lamb and the word of our testimony.

The enemy attacks churches subtly—through gossip, unresolved conflict, doctrinal drift, burnout, or pride. He delights when worship becomes performance, when leadership becomes control, when prayer becomes formality, and when discipleship becomes a program. When the church remembers its first love, when it walks in holiness and grace and treasures the gospel and reaches the lost, it becomes a beacon of light in a dark world.

Intercession is vital. Leaders must be prayed for. Families must be covered. Ministries must be birthed in prayer and sustained by it. Elders must be spiritually discerning. Worship must be Spirit-filled and truth-centred. The church's teaching must be saturated with the Word and shaped by the gospel. Only then will it have power to stand—not only against the enemy, but for the mission it has been given. The call is not merely to survive until Jesus returns. It is to contend for the faith, to proclaim the gospel, to make disciples, and to stand firm until the end. The battle is real. The cost is high. But so is the reward.

How then shall I live?

Understanding spiritual warfare is not meant to frighten us or make us experts in the demonic. It is meant to root us deeper in Christ and sharpen our awareness of the battle that rages around and within us. This chapter began by asserting that the Christian life is a battleground, not a playground.

That remains true. But it is also a battleground where the outcome has already been decided, and we are called to fight not with fear, but with faith. So how then shall I live?

Live alert but not afraid. Recognize that there is a real enemy who seeks to undermine your faith, discourage your soul, and distract your focus. But do not live in fear of him. He is already defeated. Fear gives him more ground than he has earned. Resist him, yes—but resist him as one who knows Christ has already triumphed.

Live grounded in truth. Know the Word of God. Meditate on it. Speak it. Apply it. Let it shape your identity, your decisions, and your perspective. Truth is your first and greatest defence against the lies of the enemy. Every temptation begins with a lie, and every victory begins with the truth.

Live dependent on prayer. Make prayer your lifeline, not your last resort. Pray in the Spirit on all occasions. Pray when you're strong and when you're weak. Pray for wisdom, for strength, for protection, for others. Prayer is not just preparation for battle— it is the battlefield itself.

Live submitted to God. Submission is the posture that invites power. When you walk in obedience, the enemy has no foothold. When you humble yourself under God's mighty hand, you are lifted above the reach of the accuser. Authority comes from alignment with God's will.

Live in community. Do not fight alone. Link arms with brothers and sisters in the faith. Confess your struggles. Share your burdens. Encourage one another. The enemy isolates to destroy. But God places us in a body for protection, strength, and mutual upbuilding.

Live in worship. Lift your eyes above the battle to the One who reigns. Praise breaks chains. Worship reminds your soul who is King. Even in your lowest moments, sing. The darkness cannot endure the sound of God's people declaring His glory.

Live with discernment. Not every problem is demonic, but not every struggle is just natural either. Ask God for wisdom to see what is really happening. Cultivate a Spirit-led awareness that sees beyond the surface.

Live focussed on the mission. Remember that this battle is not about you. It is about Christ and His Kingdom. Let your life bear witness to His power, His love, and His truth. Advance the gospel. Make disciples. Shine the light. Tear down strongholds — not just in your own life, but in your community, your culture, and your generation.

Above all, *live in Christ.* Abide in Him. Rest in Him. Trust in Him. He is your victory. He is your strength. He is your peace. The battle is real, but so is the presence of the risen Lord, who has said, *"Surely I am with you always, to the very end of the age."*

2. THE ORIGIN OF EVIL: THE FALL OF LUCIFER AND THE BIRTH OF REBELLION

The problem of evil

From the earliest days of human reflection, one question has haunted the heart and mind: Where did evil come from? How did a world created by a holy, good, and sovereign God come to be filled with rebellion, suffering, and death? Why do we face temptation, oppression, injustice, and pain if God is all-powerful and all-loving? These questions are not only theological — they are profoundly personal. Every act of cruelty, every broken relationship, every cancer diagnosis, and every graveyard stirs within us the ache of a fallen world. We know, instinctively, that something is terribly wrong. But how did it begin?

Scripture does not offer a tidy philosophical essay on the problem of evil. Instead, it gives us a story. A story of beauty marred by rebellion, of light overshadowed by darkness, of a garden invaded by a serpent. But before that moment in Eden — before Adam and Eve took the fateful bite — there was another fall. A fall not on earth, but in heaven. A rebellion not among humans, but among angels. To understand the full story of spiritual warfare, we must go further back — into the mystery of the unseen realm where evil was born.

Though the Bible speaks clearly about the existence of Satan and his works, it does not give a detailed chronology of his fall. Instead, it gives us glimpses — prophetic shadows, theological insights, and poetic descriptions — that, when pieced together, form a coherent picture. From passages like Isaiah 14, Ezekiel 28, and Revelation 12, we begin to see not only the origin of our adversary but the nature of his rebellion, the cause of his downfall, and the character of the evil he represents.

What we discover is sobering and essential: evil did not originate in humanity, but in angelic rebellion. Sin did not begin in the Garden of Eden, but in the heart of a glorious creature who dared to exalt himself above his Creator.

And the consequences of that rebellion now echo through every corner of creation. But even here—especially here—we must tread very carefully. We are dealing with mystery. We must not speculate where Scripture is silent, nor build dogma on poetry. Yet we must also not ignore what God has revealed. The origin of evil is not merely an academic puzzle - it is the backdrop to redemption. It is the stage upon which Christ's great victory is displayed. It is the context in which our spiritual battle unfolds.

The creation and glory of Lucifer

To understand the fall of Lucifer, we must first consider his origin. Contrary to popular imagery, Satan was not created as the prince of darkness. He was created as a being of light. In Ezekiel 28, the prophet speaks a lament over the king of Tyre—a human ruler—but the language quickly transcends all earthly categories. Many scholars believe this passage offers a dual-layered vision: both a rebuke of a proud king and a glimpse into the original fall of Satan.

In Ezekiel 28:12–14, we read, *"You were the seal of perfection, full of wisdom and perfect in beauty. You were in Eden, the garden of God… You were anointed as a guardian cherub, for so I ordained you. You were on the holy mount of God; you walked among the fiery stones."* This is not ordinary human language. It speaks of a being of extraordinary majesty and great privilege—a guardian cherub, ordained by God, dwelling in Eden and walking in the presence of divine glory.

Lucifer, whose name means "light-bringer" or "morning star," was created perfect in beauty and wisdom. He held a high position among the angelic host, likely one of the chief cherubim who served near the throne of God. His role was one of glory, worship, and guardianship. He was not created evil—he was created glorious. But his exalted position became the very seed of his downfall.

In Isaiah 14, we find another poetic oracle—this time directed at the king of Babylon. Again, the language seems to transcend the human and point to a deeper spiritual reality.

The prophet declares, *"How you have fallen from heaven, morning star, son of the dawn! You have been cast down to the earth, you who once laid low the nations!"* (Isaiah 14:12). The Hebrew term which is translated *"morning star"* is *"helel,"* which the Latin Vulgate renders as Lucifer - the only occurrence of that word in Scripture.

The passage continues: *"You said in your heart, 'I will ascend to the heavens; I will raise my throne above the stars of God... I will make myself like the Most High.'"* (Isaiah 14:13–14). Here we see the essence of Lucifer's rebellion—not ignorance, not fear, but pride. He sought to ascend. He desired not merely to serve God, but to rival Him. His heart turned from worship to ambition, from submission to self-exaltation.

This is the origin of evil. Not in some dark, chaotic force outside of God's control, but in the wilful pride of a created being who turned from the light and embraced the darkness. Lucifer wanted to be like God—but not in the way we are called to be. He wanted not godliness, but godhood. And in that moment, his glory became corruption, his wisdom became perversion, and his beauty became twisted by rebellion.

Jesus Himself affirms the reality of this fall. In Luke 10:18, He tells His disciples, *"I saw Satan fall like lightning from heaven."* This is not a metaphor. It is a declaration of history.

Satan's rebellion was real, and his expulsion from heaven was decisive. He fell from his position, from his place, from his purity. And in falling, he dragged with him others who followed his prideful path.

Revelation 12 gives us a dramatic vision: *"The great dragon was hurled down – that ancient serpent called the devil, or Satan, who leads the whole world astray. He was hurled to the earth, and his angels with him."* (Revelation 12:9). One-third of the angels, it seems, joined in his rebellion and became the demonic forces now active in the world. These are not mythical creatures, but real spiritual beings—once glorious, now fallen, and fiercely opposed to the purposes of God.

The nature of Satan's rebellion

If pride was the root of Satan's fall, deception was its fruit. In his rebellion, Lucifer not only corrupted himself but persuaded others to follow. He spread his lies in heaven before spreading them on earth. And those lies always have the same aim: to dethrone God in the hearts of His creation.

The temptation in Eden is a mirror of the rebellion in heaven. The serpent comes to Eve not with violence, but with questions. *"Did God really say…?"* (Genesis 3:1). He plants doubt. He distorts the command. He challenges the motive of God. Then he makes a promise: *"You will not certainly die… you will be like God, knowing good and evil."* (v. 4–5). The irony is thick. The very temptation that brought down Lucifer — *"I will be like the Most High"* — is now whispered into the ears of humanity.

And it worked. The same pride that corrupted the angels now enters the human heart. Eve takes the fruit, gives it to Adam, and the world fractures. But it is important to note: the serpent does not force. He entices. He deceives. He manipulates. That is his strategy still. He works not through raw power but through suggestive lies. He does not need to possess every person — he only needs to persuade them. And in a fallen world, persuasion is often enough.

Satan's rebellion is therefore ongoing. Though his initial fall was catastrophic, he continues to oppose God's purposes. He is not a passive symbol of evil — he is an active agent of it. He seeks to blind the minds of unbelievers, to accuse the saints, to tempt the faithful, and to oppose the gospel at every turn. He cannot unmake God's victory, but he can try to hinder God's people.

Yet his power is limited. He is not sovereign. He is not free to act without constraint. The book of Job reminds us that Satan needed permission to touch Job's life — and even then, God set boundaries he could not cross. In the New Testament, Jesus commands demons and they obey. The apostles cast them out in His name. And Revelation promises that a day is coming when Satan will be bound, judged, and cast forever into the lake of fire.

Until that day, the enemy rages — but he rages as a defeated foe. His fall from heaven marked the beginning of his downfall. The cross sealed his fate. And the return of Christ will bring the final blow. But for now, we live in the tension. The enemy is active. The battle is real. And we are called to stand.

The origin of evil, then, is not found in a flaw in God's creation, but in the rebellion of creatures who misused their freedom. Lucifer chose pride over worship. He chose self over submission. And in doing so, he became Satan — the adversary, the accuser, the enemy of all that is good. His fall was great, his influence is global, and his hatred of God is expressed in his hatred of God's people.

But even in this dark beginning, there is a brighter hope. God was not surprised by Satan's fall. He was not outmanoeuvred or caught off guard. The Lamb was slain from the foundation of the world. The plan of redemption was already in motion. The light shines in the darkness, and the darkness has not overcome it.

The devil's agenda in the world

While the origin of Satan lies in a singular act of rebellion in heaven, his activity did not end with his fall. In fact, the thrust of biblical history — and of spiritual warfare today — centres on his ongoing opposition to the purposes of God on earth. From the moment he deceived humanity in Eden, Satan has been at work corrupting, accusing, tempting, dividing, and destroying. Yet always within the limits God has sovereignly permitted.

Jesus referred to Satan as *"the prince of this world"* (John 12:31; 14:30), a title that describes not his legitimacy but his influence. He exercises authority — not by divine right, but by usurpation. His power operates through deception and spiritual blindness. Paul echoes this in 2 Corinthians 4:4, when he calls him *"the god of this age,"* saying that he *"has blinded the minds of unbelievers, so that they cannot see the light of the gospel that displays the glory of Christ."* This is Satan's great work: to darken the minds of men and women, preventing them from seeing the truth that sets them free.

This spiritual blindness is not an individual phenomenon—it pervades systems, cultures, ideologies, and movements. Satan is a master strategist. He shapes narratives, exalts human pride, glorifies rebellion, and normalizes sin. His influence is not always seen in grotesque evil but in subtle drift.

A society that calls evil good and good evil is one under strong spiritual delusion. In such a world, the work of the church becomes not merely missional but militant—proclaiming truth in love in a world saturated with lies.

But Satan's agenda is not limited to unbelievers. He also wages war against the people of God. The book of Revelation describes him as *"the accuser of our brothers and sisters, who accuses them before our God day and night."* (Revelation 12:10). He whispers condemnation, stirring up shame, dredging up past failures, and attempting to erode our confidence in God's grace. His accusations aim to sever our intimacy with God, to make us doubt His forgiveness and draw back from boldness in faith.

This is why one of his most common strategies is to attack our identity. If he can convince us that we are still slaves instead of sons, still condemned instead of justified, still weak instead of victorious in Christ, he can paralyze us. His lies are never abstract—they are personal, targeted, and persistent. But they are also fragile. They cannot withstand the truth. When we stand on what God has said—about Himself, about us, about the gospel—Satan's accusations fall powerless to the ground.

His other primary strategy is always temptation. James 1:14–15 describes how temptation works: *"Each person is tempted when they are dragged away by their own evil desire and enticed. Then, after desire has conceived, it gives birth to sin; and sin, when it is full-grown, gives birth to death."*

Satan entices, but he works with what is already in us. He knows our weaknesses and exploits them. He cannot force us to sin—but he can bait the hook. The more we indulge those temptations, the more power they gain. But the more we resist, the more ground we reclaim.

It's important to remember that Satan is not omnipresent. He is not personally behind every temptation or struggle. But his demonic forces — those who fell with him — continue his work. These spiritual entities operate in rebellion against God, seeking to interfere with His purposes and disrupt His people. Paul, in Ephesians 6:12, speaks of them as *"rulers... authorities... powers of this dark world... spiritual forces of evil in the heavenly realms."* They are organized, intelligent, and active. They are not omnipotent. They tremble before Christ. They flee before the authority of His name. And they will be ultimately judged by the One they defied.

Resisting the accuser: our position in Christ

If the enemy's goal is to deceive and accuse, our greatest weapon is truth. Not abstract truth, but incarnate truth — the truth of who Jesus is and who we are in Him. Spiritual warfare is not primarily about casting out demons or confronting darkness — it is about standing in our God-given identity and refusing to surrender ground to lies.

Paul's letter to the Ephesians offers a sweeping view of our position in Christ. *"God raised us up with Christ and seated us with him in the heavenly realms in Christ Jesus."* (Ephesians 2:6). This is not future tense — it is present. Spiritually, we are already seated with Christ in a place of victory and authority. We do not fight from below, but from above. The enemy is under Christ's feet — and we are in Him.

This reality changes everything. It means we do not need to fear the enemy. We need only to submit to God, resist the devil, and he will flee (James 4:7). We are not powerless. We are not victims. We are not orphans. We are children of God, indwelt by the Spirit, armed with the Word, and surrounded by the heavenly host. We stand on the unshakable foundation of Christ's finished work. But we must choose to stand. Ephesians 6 repeats the call to *"stand"* multiple times — not to attack, not to advance in aggression, but to stand firm in the face of opposition. And to stand, we must be clothed.

Paul describes the armour of God — not as mystical garb, but as a present spiritual reality. The belt of truth. The breastplate of righteousness. The gospel of peace. The shield of faith. The helmet of salvation. The sword of the Spirit. Each piece is rooted in our union with Christ.

The belt of truth secures everything else. Without truth, we are vulnerable to every lie. The breastplate of righteousness protects our hearts — not our righteousness, but Christ's imputed to us. The gospel shoes enable us to stand with readiness and proclaim peace. The shield of faith extinguishes flaming arrows — those sudden doubts, accusations, and temptations. The helmet of salvation guards our minds, reminding us who we are and to whom we belong. And the sword of the Spirit — the Word of God — is our offensive weapon, the truth that slices through deception.

To wear this armour is not a one-time ritual — it is a daily posture. It is choosing to believe what God has said rather than what we feel. It is rehearsing the truth when the enemy shouts lies. It is resisting fear with faith, accusation with grace, and temptation with Scripture. Jesus modelled this in the wilderness, answering each demonic suggestion with *"It is written."* He stood not in emotion, but in truth. And so must we.

But we do not stand alone. God has not left us defenceless. He has given us His Spirit. The Holy Spirit is not merely a comforter — He is a warrior. He intercedes for us, empowers us, convicts us, guides us, and strengthens us. When we pray in the Spirit, we engage the battle not in the flesh but with divine power. We are not left to our own strategies. We are filled with the very presence of God.

This is why walking by the Spirit is the most strategic form of spiritual warfare. Paul contrasts the works of the flesh with the fruit of the Spirit in Galatians 5. When we walk in the Spirit, we produce love, joy, peace, patience, kindness, goodness, faithfulness, gentleness, and self-control. These are not passive virtues — they are active weapons.

Every time we love in the face of hatred, rejoice in affliction, show patience in provocation, we resist the enemy. Spiritual fruit is spiritual resistance. And when we stumble—and we will—we must run not from God, but to Him. The enemy's accusations thrive in the darkness of secrecy and shame. But when we confess our sin, God is faithful and just to forgive and to cleanse us from all unrighteousness. The blood of Jesus is not just for conversion—it is for communion. It is the constant covering by which we live and breathe and fight.

Angels, demons, and the cosmic conflict

One of the lesser understood dimensions of spiritual warfare is the role of angels and demons in the cosmic conflict. Scripture presents a reality in which heavenly beings are engaged in a struggle far beyond our sight but not beyond our involvement.

Angels are ministering spirits, sent to serve those who will inherit salvation (Hebrews 1:14). They are not winged humans or chubby cherubs. They are mighty warriors, messengers, and worshipers of God. They protect, deliver, and engage in battles on behalf of God's purposes. In Daniel 10, the prophet prays for 21 days before receiving an answer. When the angel arrives, he explains that he was delayed by a demonic *"prince of Persia"* until the archangel Michael came to assist. This extraordinary passage offers a rare window into the spiritual resistance that can occur in the heavenly realms.

Demons, by contrast, are fallen angels—those who joined Lucifer in his rebellion. They operate in deception, fear, and bondage. During Jesus' earthly ministry, He regularly confronted and expelled them. The Gospels are filled with stories of demonic possession, oppression, and influence. Jesus never treated these encounters as metaphorical. He spoke, and they obeyed. He commanded, and they fled.

But it's important to note that not all spiritual warfare is about demons. While demonic influence is real, it is not the explanation for every struggle. We must be discerning. Some battles are internal—fleshly desires, sinful habits, unrenewed minds.

Others are cultural — worldly patterns and pressures that pull us from the truth. And yes, some are direct demonic interference. But in each case, the response is the same: truth, prayer, obedience, and the presence of Christ.

In the early church, believers confronted demonic power not with rituals, but with authority. In Acts 16, Paul casts out a spirit of divination from a slave girl. In Acts chapter 19, God does some extraordinary miracles through Paul, and evil spirits are expelled. Yet the sons of Sceva, who attempt to use Jesus' name without knowing Him, are overwhelmed by a demonic man. Authority in spiritual warfare is not in words, but in relationship. The enemy knows those who walk with God.

This is a key principle: spiritual authority flows from intimacy with Christ. It is not a technique. It is not volume. It is not charisma. It is the fruit of abiding. When we know Him, we carry His name — not as a magic word, but as a mark of identity. When we are filled with His Spirit, we carry His presence. And the enemy cannot withstand the presence of the risen Christ.

The final outcome of this cosmic conflict is not in doubt. Revelation describes the devil being thrown into the lake of fire, where he will be tormented forever (Revelation 20:10). His rebellion ends in defeat. His accusations will cease. His deception will be exposed. But until that day, the battle rages. And we are caught in the tension — redeemed, but still at war.

Yet we do not fight alone. And we do not fight uncertainly. Christ is our King. The Spirit is our helper. The Word is our sword. The church is our family. And the victory is assured.

The mystery of God's sovereignty and Satan's defeat

As we trace the origin of evil through the fall of Lucifer and the rise of rebellion, a deeper and often more difficult question emerges: If God is sovereign, why did He allow such a being to rebel? Why would a perfect Creator allow pride to infect His creation?

Why did God permit Satan to tempt Adam and Eve, knowing the catastrophic consequences? And why has God not yet brought final judgment upon the devil and his works?

These are not small questions, nor are they entirely answerable from our limited perspective. Yet Scripture offers signposts — truths that anchor us even when mystery remains. The first is that God's sovereignty is never compromised by the presence of evil. Satan may rage, but he does so on a leash. He is powerful, but never supreme. He is cunning, but never autonomous. The Lord remains enthroned above all, working even through opposition to fulfil His ultimate purpose.

Romans 8:28 affirms that *"in all things God works for the good of those who love him, who have been called according to his purpose."* "All things" includes spiritual warfare, temptation, testing, and even Satan's schemes. Joseph's words to his brothers in Genesis 50 ring true across all time: *"You intended to harm me, but God intended it for good to accomplish what is now being done."* Satan's rebellion did not derail God's plan — it became a backdrop against which His justice, mercy, and glory would shine more brightly.

This does not make God the author of evil, but it does affirm His absolute rule over it. Satan is not a rival god — he is a rebellious creature. He is not an equal force in a cosmic dualism — he is a defeated foe whose every move unwittingly serves the greater glory of God. Even the cross, Satan's apparent moment of triumph, was his undoing. As 1 Corinthians 2:8 states, *"None of the rulers of this age understood it, for if they had, they would not have crucified the Lord of glory."*

The delay in Satan's final judgment is not evidence of divine weakness, but of divine patience. God is giving time for repentance, for the gospel to go forth, for His people to grow and shine in the midst of darkness. Revelation makes clear that the day is coming when the devil, the beast, and the false prophet will be cast into the lake of fire. That judgment is certain. But in the meantime, the battlefield remains active.

And we are called to walk faithfully, knowing the outcome but still engaged in the conflict. This tension—between the now and the not yet, between the victory of the cross and the final consummation—is the space in which all spiritual warfare occurs. Satan is defeated, yet active. The Kingdom is present yet advancing. The war is won, yet the battle continues. And this paradox is not meant to confuse us, but to compel us to live with urgency, hope, and spiritual sobriety.

Lessons from the fall of Lucifer

The fall of Lucifer is not only a theological doctrine; it is a cautionary tale. It is a mirror held up to the human heart. The pride that brought down an archangel is the same pride that lurks in all of us. The desire to be like God—to define our own truth, to pursue our own glory, to exalt our will above His—did not die in Eden. It lives on in every heart that has not been fully surrendered to Christ.

Isaiah 14 captures the essence of Lucifer's rebellion in five bold declarations: *"I will ascend... I will raise... I will sit enthroned... I will ascend... I will make myself like the Most High."* The repetition is deliberate. The centre of Satan's fall was the exaltation of self. He turned inward when he was created to gaze upward. He grasped at a throne that was never his. And in doing so, he lost everything.

Pride remains the root of much spiritual defeat today. It disguises itself as ambition, self-confidence, independence, or even religious zeal. But at its core, pride dethrones God and enthrones self. It resists correction, refuses submission, and rejects dependence. It isolates, corrupts, and blinds. It is no wonder that James writes, *"God opposes the proud but shows favour to the humble."* (James 4:6). Pride not only opens the door to the enemy—it aligns us with him.

Conversely, humility is our greatest protection. It was humility that marked Christ, who *"did not consider equality with God something to be used to his own advantage... he humbled himself by becoming obedient to death."* (Philippians 2:6–8).

And it is humility that must mark us. The humble heart is teachable, dependent, and yielded. It stands not in its own strength but in the grace of God. And that grace, Peter assures us, is sufficient: *"Humble yourselves, therefore, under God's mighty hand, that he may lift you up in due time."* (1 Peter 5:6).

Lucifer's fall also teaches us the danger of spiritual complacency. He was not tempted from without—his fall began from within. And it happened in the very presence of God. This is sobering. It means that external religion is no guarantee of internal devotion. One can be near the throne and far from the King. One can lead in worship and still harbour rebellion. It is not our position that keeps us safe, but our posture.

This should instil in us a holy fear—not terror, but reverence. The fear of the Lord is the beginning of wisdom. It keeps us from presumption, protects us from arrogance, and draws us into deeper dependence. It reminds us that apart from Christ, we are vulnerable—but in Christ, we are secure.

Finally, Lucifer's fall warns us of the cost of rebellion. His trajectory was from heaven to earth to judgment. His path was downward, his end is destruction. No rebellion against God ends well. No lie of the enemy leads to freedom. Sin always promises what it cannot deliver. It always takes more than it gives. And it always leads to death.

But thanks be to God, we are not without hope. What Lucifer lost in pride, we gain through grace. What he destroyed in rebellion, Christ restores through redemption. We need not fear his power—we need only follow our King.

How then shall I live?

The fall of Lucifer and the birth of evil is not just an ancient tragedy or a theological mystery—it is a living backdrop to our daily discipleship. It explains the conflict we feel within ourselves, the deception we see in the world, and the resistance we encounter when we pursue the things of God. But it also anchors our hope.

For the One who saw Satan fall like lightning has given us power to tread on serpents and to overcome every scheme of the enemy. So how then shall I live?

Live with theological clarity. Understand that Satan is real, fallen, active, and defeated. He is not a myth, not a metaphor, and not invincible. He is a created being, operating under the sovereignty of God, and destined for judgment. Let the Scriptures - not speculation - shape your view of him.

Live in humility. Pride is the soil in which rebellion grows. Guard your heart. Refuse to exalt yourself. Walk in dependence on God, acknowledging your need for His grace. The humble are lifted up. The proud are brought low. Remember that Lucifer fell not because of weakness, but because of ambition without submission.

Live with discernment. The devil masquerades as an angel of light. Not all that glitters is from God. Not all spiritual activity is holy. Test every spirit. Hold fast to what is good. Be slow to trust appearances and quick to compare everything with the Word of God.

Live in your God-given identity. Satan's goal is to undermine who you are in Christ. Don't give him that ground. Stand firm in the truth that you are forgiven, adopted, empowered, and victorious in Jesus. Clothe yourself daily in the armour of God. Let truth guard your mind and righteousness protect your heart.

Live with gospel confidence. The cross has disarmed the enemy. The resurrection has sealed his fate. You do not fight for victory — you fight from it. Walk in the authority Christ has given you. Speak truth boldly. Resist the enemy without fear. And never forget that greater is He who is in you than he who is in the world.

Live with vigilance. The devil prowls like a roaring lion, seeking someone to devour. Be alert. Stay awake. Guard your heart, your thoughts, your relationships, your doctrine. Don't be naïve. The battle is real. But so is your protection in Christ.

Live submitted to God. Submission is not weakness — it is strength under covering. When you yield to God, you place yourself under His protection and provision. Submission precedes resistance. Authority flows from obedience.

Live with eternal perspective. This war will not last forever. Satan's time is short. Christ will return. Justice will be done. The deceiver will be silenced. And the Kingdom will come in fullness. Until that day, hold the line. Proclaim the truth. Fight the good fight. And know that your labour in the Lord is never in vain.

In a world which is shaped by rebellion, let your life be shaped by surrender. In a culture ruled by pride, let humility be your banner. In a battle marked by lies, let truth be your weapon. And in the shadow of the fall, let your light shine — bearing witness to the grace that redeems, the power that delivers, and the King who reigns.

3. THE NATURE AND POWER OF SATAN: WHAT THE BIBLE REALLY TEACHES

Naming the enemy: Who is Satan?

For many Christians, the idea of Satan evokes vague imagery — a red creature with horns, a tail, and a pitchfork. Others envision an evil force lurking in the shadows, whispering temptation into our ears or lurking behind disasters and moral decline. But for all the cultural caricatures, there remains a pressing need to ask: who is Satan really, according to the Bible? What does Scripture actually teach — not about mythology or metaphor, but about the true nature and power of our adversary?

The Bible speaks often and clearly about Satan, using a wide array of names and titles that reveal his character and mission. He is not a fictional symbol of evil; he is a real, personal being with intellect, emotion, will, and strategy. He is introduced in the earliest chapters of Scripture and remains active until the closing scenes of Revelation. To understand spiritual warfare and to walk in truth, we must know our enemy — not in morbid fascination, but in sober awareness.

The name *"Satan"* itself means *"adversary"* or *"accuser."* He first appears by name in the book of Job, where he comes before God and challenges the sincerity of Job's righteousness. In that context, Satan functions as a kind of prosecuting attorney — accusing Job, questioning his motives, and seeking permission to test him. The name reveals his nature: he is fundamentally against God and against God's people. He opposes, he resists, he slanders, and he accuses.

Another prominent title is *"the devil,"* from the Greek *diabolos,* meaning *"slanderer"* or *"false accuser."* This term emphasises his deceptive and malicious speech. Jesus refers to him as *"a liar and the father of lies"* (John 8:44), revealing that his power is rooted not in brute strength, but in deception. From the beginning, Satan's chief strategy has been to twist the truth, to plant doubt, and to distort God's Word.

He is also called *"the tempter"* (Matthew 4:3), *"the evil one"* (Matthew 13:19), *"the prince of this world"* (John 12:31), *"the god of this age"* (2 Corinthians 4:4), and *"the ruler of the kingdom of the air"* (Ephesians 2:2). Each of these titles emphasises different aspects of his work: his influence over worldly systems, his capacity to blind and deceive, his desire to rule through darkness and fear.

Perhaps most vividly, Revelation 12 refers to him as *"the great dragon... that ancient serpent called the devil, or Satan, who leads the whole world astray."* This image pulls together the serpent of Genesis 3, the adversary of Job, and the dragon of apocalyptic judgment. He is not to be underestimated. But neither is he to be glorified.

The Bible never portrays Satan as God's equal, nor as an omnipresent or omniscient force. He is a created being, finite and doomed, yet permitted — for a time — to oppose the purposes of God.

Created, fallen, and limited

One of the most important theological truths about Satan is that he is a created being. He was made by God — originally good, as were all things in creation. He is not eternal, not self-existent, and not sovereign. Colossians 1:16 says of Christ, *"For in him all things were created: things in heaven and on earth, visible and invisible, whether thrones or powers or rulers or authorities; all things have been created through him and for him."* This includes the angelic realm, of which Satan was once a part.

As we saw in Chapter 2, Satan was likely a high-ranking angel who fell through pride, desiring to usurp the authority of God. His fall was self-inflicted. There was no external temptation — only an internal corruption of ambition and self-exaltation. Isaiah 14 and Ezekiel 28, while directed at earthly kings, offer poetic windows into this rebellion. The picture is of a being created with glory and purpose, who rejected that purpose in pursuit of his own throne.

But with that fall came limitation. Satan is not everywhere. He is not all-knowing. He is not all-powerful. He cannot read minds, control the future, or act independently of divine permission. His knowledge is vast, but not infinite. His influence is real, but not boundless.

In Job 1 and 2, we see that Satan requires God's permission to touch Job's life—and even then, God sets strict boundaries. He may test, but only within the limits God allows.

This truth brings comfort and confidence. Satan is dangerous, yes—but he is also restrained. He prowls like a roaring lion, seeking whom he may devour (1 Peter 5:8), but he does not prowl without leash. God is sovereign. The devil rages, but only within the parameters that serve God's greater redemptive plan.

That then raises another mystery: *Why does God permit Satan to continue his activity at all?* Why allow such a being to wreak havoc, deceive, tempt, and destroy? The answer, while not fully explained, points us to the sovereignty and wisdom of God. Scripture consistently shows that God uses even the schemes of the enemy to accomplish His purposes.

In the story of Job, Satan's attack results in deeper faith and greater revelation. In the wilderness, Jesus' temptation becomes a platform to reveal His obedience and authority. At the cross, Satan's apparent triumph becomes his ultimate defeat. And in our lives, trials and temptations refine our character, draw us to prayer, and teach us dependence. What Satan means for harm, God uses for good. Satan is a pawn in the hand of providence—resisting God's plan, yet unwittingly serving it.

What Satan can and cannot do

A key part of spiritual maturity is learning to rightly discern the scope of Satan's power. Many Christians fall into one of two extremes—either dismissing his existence entirely, or attributing to him far more power than he actually possesses. But Scripture helps us walk the middle path, acknowledging his activity without exaggerating it.

What can Satan do?

He can tempt (Matthew 4:1). He can lie (John 8:44). He can accuse (Revelation 12:10). He can also blind the minds of unbelievers (2 Corinthians 4:4). He can hinder our plans and ministries (1 Thessalonians 2:18). He can oppress and harass; he can even masquerade as an angel of light (2 Corinthians 12:7; 11:14). He can incite division, pride, and discouragement. He can also inhabit people who surrender themselves fully to his influence (Luke 22:3; Acts 5:3). And through his demonic forces, he can exert real influence in the lives of individuals, churches, and even nations.

What can Satan not do?

He cannot create. He cannot forgive. He cannot love. He cannot compel a believer to sin. He cannot separate us from the love of God. He cannot possess a Christian indwelt by the Holy Spirit. He cannot act apart from divine permission. He cannot resist the name of Jesus spoken in faith. And he cannot change the fact that his time is short, his judgment is certain, and his destiny is sealed.

1 John 4:4 offers a vital assurance: *"You, dear children, are from God and have overcome them, because the one who is in you is greater than the one who is in the world."* That single truth must govern all our thinking about Satan. He is not greater. He is not victorious. He is not to be feared in the same way we revere God. Yes, we take him seriously. Yes, we resist him. But we do so knowing that the power within us — Christ Himself — is infinitely greater.

One of Satan's cleverest tricks is to hide behind extremes. He thrives when Christians dismiss him as irrelevant. But he also thrives when they obsess over him — blaming him for every setback, every temptation, inconvenience and poor choice!

When believers live in fear of curses, spirits, generational bonds, or demonic presence under every rock, they are walking not in faith but in superstition. Spiritual warfare becomes distorted. The focus shifts from Christ to the devil, from truth to spectacle, from Scripture to experience.

What Scripture teaches us is balance. Awareness without obsession. Confidence without arrogance. Discernment without fear. We are not told to chase demons, name territorial spirits, or develop elaborate rituals. We are told to resist the devil, to be alert, to stand firm, and to walk in the light.

James 4:7 captures the essence of the Christian posture toward Satan: *"Submit yourselves, then, to God. Resist the devil, and he will flee from you."* Submission to God is the foundation. Resistance follows. Victory is promised. This is not mystical — it is practical. When we walk in obedience, when we live in truth, when we remain in fellowship with God and His people, we are protected. The devil flees not from our strength, but from the One who stands with us.

The schemes of the devil

Paul's warning in Ephesians 6:11 is urgent and specific: *"Put on the full armour of God, so that you can take your stand against the devil's schemes."* The Greek word for "schemes" (*methodeia*) suggests craftiness, deceit, and deliberate strategy. Satan is not haphazard in his attacks. He studies, plans, and implements targeted assaults against individuals, churches, and nations. To ignore his strategies is to walk into battle blind and unarmed.

One of the most effective strategies Satan employs is deception. Jesus called him "the father of lies" (John 8:44), and his primary weapon is falsehood. This doesn't always look like blatant contradiction of truth; more often, it comes as distortion. Satan rarely tells outright lies. He prefers half-truths, twisted Scripture, and subtle reframing.

In the Garden of Eden, he did not begin by denying God's word, but by questioning it: *"Did God really say…?"* (Genesis 3:1). This approach undermines confidence in God's character and introduces doubt where faith once stood. Deception leads to disorientation. When believers begin to base their lives on feelings, experience, or cultural norms instead of God's Word, they become susceptible to every wind of doctrine and trend of the age.

This is how the enemy infiltrates churches — not through frontal attacks, but through a slow erosion of truth. Doctrinal compromise, moral relativism, and spiritual apathy are often the fruit of seeds planted by deceit.

Another scheme is accusation. Revelation 12:10 calls Satan *"the accuser of our brothers and sisters, who accuses them before our God day and night."* These accusations are designed to produce shame, guilt, and despair. He will remind us of past failures, exaggerate our weaknesses, and whisper in our mind that we are disqualified, unforgivable, or unusable by God. He seeks to cripple our confidence and sever our intimacy with Christ.

But Scripture reminds us that *"there is now no condemnation for those who are in Christ Jesus"* (Romans 8:1). The blood of Christ silences every accusation. When we stand on that truth, the accuser loses his voice. His words may come — but they have no legal ground. We are justified. We are cleansed. We are adopted. And no charge can stick in the courtroom of grace.

Satan also employs temptation as a key tactic. Temptation is not sin — but it is the threshold where sin waits. James 1:14-15 explains the process: *"Each person is tempted when they are dragged away by their own evil desire and enticed. Then, after desire has conceived, it gives birth to sin."* Satan entices by appealing to desires already present within us. He does not create new desires — he exploits disordered ones.

This is why spiritual warfare is not just about resisting external attack but about cultivating internal holiness. A pure heart is the best defence against temptation. The devil may bait the hook, but he relies on something in us to bite. When we walk closely with the Spirit, when we renew our minds with truth, when we practice confession and accountability, we close the doors he would otherwise enter.

Division is another of Satan's favourite tools. Jesus prayed that His followers would be one (John 17:21), knowing that unity reflects the nature of God and draws people to the gospel.

But Satan sows discord — through offense, unforgiveness, gossip, and pride. He loves when Christians fight each other instead of fighting him. He delights in factions, theological quarrels, personality-driven churches, and leadership conflicts.

Paul warned the Corinthians not to be *"outwitted by Satan. For we are not unaware of his schemes"* (2 Corinthians 2:11). The context? A call to forgive and restore a repentant brother. Satan's scheme was not some dramatic demonic event — it was the lingering of unforgiveness in a fractured community. When we harbour bitterness, hold grudges, or refuse reconciliation, we give Satan a foothold. The greatest spiritual warfare sometimes looks like saying, "I forgive you."

Another scheme is fear. Fear paralyzes. Fear exaggerates. Fear fixates. It makes us shrink back from obedience, isolate from community, and question God's promises. When Peter tried to walk on water, it was fear that caused him to sink. When Israel stood before the Promised Land, it was fear that kept them out. Fear doesn't need facts — it only needs imagination. And Satan is a master at planting fearful scenarios and worst-case outcomes in the mind.

But Scripture offers a simple remedy: *"Perfect love drives out fear"* (1 John 4:18). The more we abide in the love of God, the less room fear has to breathe. We cannot stop fearful thoughts from arriving — but we can refuse to entertain them. We can take them captive and submit them to Christ. When fear knocks, faith answers.

Discerning the devil's voice

One of the most pressing needs in the church today is the cultivation of discernment. In a world flooded with voices — spiritual, emotional, cultural — it is easy to become confused. But Scripture calls us to test every spirit (1 John 4:1), to examine everything and hold fast to what is good (1 Thessalonians 5:21). Discernment is not suspicion. It is not cynicism. It is the Spirit-enabled ability to distinguish truth from error, light from darkness, the voice of the Shepherd from the voice of the thief.

So how do we recognize the devil's voice? He speaks through lies, shame, confusion, and condemnation. His words isolate, discourage, distort, and destroy. They produce restlessness, panic, and doubt. They elevate self and minimize Christ. They lead us toward hiddenness, secrecy, and compromise.

By contrast, the voice of God is marked by truth, peace, clarity, and conviction. It draws us to repentance without despair. It exposes sin without crushing hope. It leads to worship, freedom, and intimacy. God's voice aligns with Scripture, honours Jesus, and bears the fruit of the Spirit. It never contradicts His Word and never leads us away from the body of Christ.

The more familiar we are with God's voice, the more quickly we'll recognize the counterfeit. This is why immersion in the Word is essential. The Bible is not just our sword in warfare — it is our filter in confusion. It trains our spiritual senses, sharpens our discernment, and anchors our hearts in what is unchanging.

Satan also speaks through systems and culture. His influence is not limited to personal temptation. He weaves lies into media, politics, education, and entertainment. He normalizes what is evil and mocks what is holy. He champions self-expression over submission, feelings over truth, and autonomy over obedience. The church must be awake to these dynamics — not to be combative, but to be discerning. We cannot afford to drift with the tide. We must be anchored in truth.

Sometimes the devil's voice is loud and aggressive. Other times, it is quiet and reasonable. That's the danger. He comes as an angel of light (2 Corinthians 11:14). He quotes Scripture (Matthew 4:6). He offers shortcuts to glory, and compromises wrapped in piety. If we are not discerning, we will be deceived not by obvious evil, but by convincing imitations of good.

Discernment is not optional — it is essential. Especially in a world of spiritual confusion, celebrity ministries, viral teachings, and theological drift. The enemy will always exploit the absence of discernment. But those who walk closely with the Shepherd will know His voice — and will follow Him.

Bound but active: living in the tension

Perhaps one of the greatest theological tensions regarding Satan is this: he is defeated—yet he is active. Christ's death and resurrection decisively broke the power of the enemy. Colossians 2:15 says that Christ *"disarmed the powers and authorities, he made a public spectacle of them, triumphing over them by the cross."* This is not partial victory—it is total triumph.

And yet, the New Testament still calls us to vigilance. Peter warns us that Satan *"prowls around like a roaring lion looking for someone to devour"* (1 Peter 5:8). Paul says we are still engaged in a struggle *"against the powers of this dark world and against the spiritual forces of evil in the heavenly realms"* (Ephesians 6:12). Revelation speaks of the devil waging war against the saints (Revelation 12:17). How can these things be true if Christ has already won?

The answer lies in the tension between the already and the not yet of God's Kingdom. Satan has been defeated in principle but not yet destroyed in presence. His authority has been broken, but his activity persists. His future is sealed, but his influence remains—for now. We live between D-Day and V-Day, to borrow the language of military history. The decisive battle has been won, but the final cleanup is still underway.

This tension calls us to faith-filled vigilance. We must neither live as though Satan has no power, nor as though he has ultimate power. He is a defeated foe, but he is still a real one. His wounds are mortal, but his rage is intense. Like a dying animal, he thrashes violently, trying to do as much damage as he can before the end.

This also explains why deliverance and healing can be real, yet the battle can return. Victory today does not mean immunity tomorrow. Spiritual warfare is not a one-time event—it is a lifestyle of dependence, discernment, and obedience. Just as the Israelites had to possess the land little by little, so we walk in freedom one step at a time. The enemy may retreat, but he often returns to test the gates.

But we are not powerless. We are not unequipped. In Christ, we have everything we need to stand. We have His authority, His Spirit, His Word, His armour, and His body—the church. When we live in communion with Him and in fellowship with one another, we become a fortress against the enemy's schemes.

And we have one weapon the enemy cannot mimic: the blood of the Lamb. Revelation 12:11 declares, *"They triumphed over him by the blood of the Lamb and by the word of their testimony."* This is the foundation of all spiritual victory. The blood of Jesus is not just a symbol—it is the legal basis by which Satan is disarmed and defeated. It cleanses our conscience, cancels our debt, and silences every accusation.

Our testimony matters too—not merely our words, but our lives. Every time we walk in freedom, every time we choose faith over fear, every time we forgive instead of retaliating, we declare that the devil has lost. Our lives become living proof that Christ is King, and the enemy's grip is broken.

Satan's activity in the church

One of the enemy's most sinister and devastating tactics is his attempt to infiltrate and undermine the Church itself. While many believers imagine Satan's work as something overtly evil, most of his most effective operations happen quietly within the community of faith.

Paul warned the Corinthian believers of this danger, saying, *"Satan himself masquerades as an angel of light. It is not surprising, then, if his servants also masquerade as servants of righteousness."* (2 Corinthians 11:14–15). The implication is sobering, not every teacher who uses the name of Jesus is sent by Him.

Satan attacks the church in many different ways: through false doctrine, moral compromise, division, and just spiritual apathy. Paul says in 1 Timothy 4:1, that *"some will abandon the faith and follow deceiving spirits and things taught by demons."* That's a strong warning.

There are teachings circulating in the Church today that originate not merely in human error, but in demonic influence. They may appear to be biblical, they may sound compassionate, or seem progressive, but if they distort the gospel or deny Christ's lordship, they serve the enemy's agenda.

Moral compromise is another subtle but deadly weapon. Satan lures leaders into sin to discredit their witness and devastate their congregations. He feeds a culture of hiddenness and hypocrisy, where image matters more than integrity. When leaders fall, it reinforces cynicism and discouragement in the body of Christ. That's why Scripture calls pastors and elders to lives of visible, consistent holiness — not because they are perfect, but because the Church is especially vulnerable to corruption from the top.

Division could arguably be Satan's favourite scheme. The New Testament repeatedly exhorts believers to unity because the enemy is constantly seeking to fracture the body of Christ. Whether through petty disagreements, ethnic or cultural pride, personality conflicts, or doctrinal legalism, Satan delights when Christians draw battle lines against one another. Jesus said, "If a house is divided against itself, that house cannot stand" (Mark 3:25). When the Church fights itself, it ceases to fight the real enemy.

Finally, spiritual apathy can sap the church of its power. When Christians grow lukewarm, become prayerless, distracted, and comfortable, they cease to be a threat. Satan doesn't need to destroy a church outright if he can simply make it irrelevant. A congregation that conforms to the world, ignores the Word, and neglects the poor may still bear the name of Jesus but lack His power.

To guard against these strategies, the Church must be discerning, prayerful, and deeply rooted in Scripture. Leadership must be accountable. Doctrine must be sound. Worship must be Christ-centred. Fellowship must be honest. And every believer must take seriously their role in the health and holiness of the body.

The defeat of Satan and the final victory of Christ

While much of this chapter has focused on the reality and danger of Satan, it would be incomplete without declaring his absolute defeat and the ultimate victory of Jesus Christ. The Bible is clear: Satan is not only opposed to God—he is also overthrown by Him.

At the cross, Jesus delivered the decisive blow to the enemy. Colossians 2:15 says, "*And having disarmed the powers and authorities, he made a public spectacle of them, triumphing over them by the cross.*" What appeared to be Satan's greatest victory—the death of the Son of God—was, in fact, his greatest defeat. In dying, Christ satisfied the justice of God, broke the curse of sin, and nullified the legal claims of the enemy over humanity.

Hebrews 2:14 says, "*Since the children have flesh and blood, he too shared in their humanity so that by his death he might break the power of him who holds the power of death – that is, the devil.*" Through His resurrection, Jesus conquered the grave and stripped Satan of his ultimate weapon: the fear of death. Now, for the believer, death is no longer a prison but a passage.

But Satan's final destruction is still to come. Revelation 20 describes a day when the devil will be bound, judged, and cast into the lake of fire: "*And the devil, who deceived them, was thrown into the lake of burning sulphur*" (Revelation 20:10). There will be no resurrection for Satan. His story ends in isolation and ruin. Evil will not endure. The deceiver will be silenced forever.

Until that day, the Church lives in the in-between—armed with the victory of Christ, yet still engaged in battle. This is not cause for fear, but for vigilance. We fight from victory, not for it. The outcome is settled, but the skirmishes continue. And in these skirmishes, the Church learns to rely on the strength of Christ, the power of His Spirit, and the truth of His Word.

That is why Paul closes his letter to the Romans with these hopeful words: "*The God of peace will soon crush Satan under your feet. The grace of our Lord Jesus be with you.*" (Romans 16:20).

How then shall I live?

Given the biblical truth about the nature and power of Satan, how should the believer live? How can we navigate life in this spiritual battlefield without falling into fear, denial, or obsession? Here are some guiding principles that emerge from Scripture:

Live alert, not afraid. Peter's command is clear: *"Be alert and of sober mind. Your enemy the devil prowls around like a roaring lion looking for someone to devour."* (1 Peter 5:8). Spiritual warfare requires vigilance. We must be aware of the enemy's tactics and resist his schemes. But this alertness is never fear-based. Our awareness is grounded in faith, not paranoia. Satan is real, but Christ is greater.

Stay rooted in truth. Jesus prayed to the Father, *"Sanctify them by the truth; your word is truth."* (John 17:17). The most powerful defence against the enemy's lies is a mind renewed by Scripture. Christians who neglect the Word are vulnerable to deception. But those who treasure it, meditate on it, and live by it walk in discernment and strength.

Walk in obedience and repentance. James 4:7 offers the sequence for victory: *"Submit yourselves, then, to God. Resist the devil, and he will flee from you."* Submission always comes first. Obedience to God undercuts the enemy's influence. Sin gives Satan a foothold; repentance takes it away. We must be quick to confess, quick to forgive, and quick to obey.

Stand in your identity. Satan's accusations lose power when we remember who we are in Christ. We are forgiven, chosen, adopted, sealed, empowered, and protected. We do not fight for victory; we fight from it. Knowing our identity as children of God gives us confidence to resist the lies of the enemy.

Cultivate spiritual disciplines. Prayer, worship, fasting, fellowship, and Scripture reading are not religious routines—they are weapons of war. They draw us closer to God, build our faith, and expose the enemy's tactics.

Paul urges believers to *"pray in the Spirit on all occasions with all kinds of prayers and requests."* (Ephesians 6:18). The battlefield is often won in the secret place.

Stay connected to the body. Lone Christians are easy targets. God has placed us in the Church for mutual strength, correction, encouragement, and accountability. When we isolate ourselves, we become vulnerable. But when we walk in community, we are stronger together. We cover each other, stand with each other, and remind each other of the truth.

Keep your eyes on Jesus. Ultimately, spiritual warfare is not about the devil — it is about Christ. The focus is not on the battle, but on the Victor. Hebrews 12:2 calls us to fix our eyes on Jesus, *"the pioneer and perfecter of faith."* As we gaze on Him alone, we are transformed. As we trust Him, we are secured. As we follow Him, we are protected.

Spiritual warfare is real. The enemy is active. But the King is on the throne. Satan trembles at the name of Jesus, and that name has been given to us. Let us walk in truth, stand in grace, resist in faith, and live in victory.

1 John 4:4 *"The one who is in you is greater than the one who is in the world."*

4. THE DEMONIC REALM: UNDERSTANDING THE ROLE OF EVIL SPIRITS TODAY

Unseen but active: demons in the biblical worldview

The Bible presents a world that is not merely physical, but spiritual. From Genesis to Revelation, we are shown a reality in which angelic and demonic beings interact with human affairs.

For the biblical writers, demons were not metaphors for psychological distress or mythological figures inherited from pagan lore—they were real, personal, malevolent beings who oppose God and afflict His people.

The New Testament assumes the presence and activity of demons as part of everyday life. Jesus routinely encountered and expelled demons during His earthly ministry. His apostles continued this pattern. The early Church was born into a context of spiritual conflict, and its leaders were not strangers to confrontations with dark powers. To embrace a biblical worldview is to accept the existence of evil spirits and to understand their place in the larger drama of redemption.

Paul offers a stark reminder in Ephesians 6:12: *"For our struggle is not against flesh and blood, but against the rulers, against the authorities, against the powers of this dark world and against the spiritual forces of evil in the heavenly realms."* This verse dismantles the modern secular assumption that all problems have natural causes. It also warns us against a reductionist Christianity that has no room for the spiritual dimension of evil.

What, then, are demons? The Bible does not really give us a comprehensive demonology, but it does offer enough detail for us to sketch a clear picture. We see in Revelation 12:4, 2 Peter 2:4, that demons are fallen angels, created beings who joined Satan in his rebellion against God. They are spiritual, not physical. They possess intelligence, will, and emotion. They recognize Jesus' authority (Luke 8:28), they can speak (Mark 5:9), and they desire embodiment (Matthew 12:43–45).

Their purpose is singular: to oppose the will of God and to destroy the image of God within humanity. Whether through deception, oppression, possession, or manipulation, demons work to spread darkness wherever they are allowed influence. They are not all-powerful — but they are dangerous. They are not everywhere — but they are active. And they are not to be dismissed lightly.

Demonic possession and oppression: what's the difference?

An important distinction we need to make in understanding demonic activity is the definitive difference between possession and oppression. These terms are sometimes confused or used interchangeably, but they describe very different realities.

Demonic possession refers to the state in which an evil spirit takes up residence within a person, exerting control over their speech, actions, and even personality. In Scripture, we see this clearly in cases like the Gerasene demoniac (Mark 5:1–20), whose behaviour was destructive, violent, and uncontrollable. He lived among the tombs, cried out day and night, and could not be restrained. When Jesus asked for the demon's name, the reply was chilling: "*My name is Legion, for we are many.*"

Possession is severe. It involves the invasion of a person's body and often brings with it physical torment, psychological confusion, social isolation, and spiritual bondage. In all biblical cases of possession, deliverance required direct confrontation and the authoritative command of Christ or His apostles. There is no indication that natural remedies, counselling, or religious ritual alone were sufficient. Only the power of God could expel such forces.

It's important to note that the New Testament never presents believers in Christ as being demon-possessed. The indwelling of the Holy Spirit and the indwelling of a demon are mutually exclusive realities. While Christians can be tempted, deceived, and oppressed, they cannot be possessed. Possession is the domain of those outside the kingdom of God.

Demonic oppression, however, is a broader and more common phenomenon. It refers to any external influence, harassment, or affliction by demonic forces. Oppression can take many forms: persistent temptation, irrational fear, spiritual heaviness, disturbing dreams, compulsive behaviour, relational strife, and more. It may be momentary or prolonged, subtle or intense.

Even faithful Christians can experience demonic oppression. Paul spoke of a *"thorn in the flesh, a messenger of Satan"* which had tormented him (2 Corinthians 12:7). While we do not know exactly what this was, it demonstrates that demonic harassment is possible even for those walking closely with God. In fact, it is often those making the greatest impact for the kingdom who experience the fiercest resistance.

Oppression does not mean failure. It is not always the result of personal sin. Sometimes it is actually the backlash of obedience. Sometimes it is a wake-up call to engage in prayer and fasting. Sometimes it is a call to stand firm and resist the devil, knowing that he will flee (James 4:7).

Distinguishing between possession and oppression helps prevent two errors: on one side, the fear that every struggle is a sign of demonic control; on the other, the ignorance that dismisses demonic involvement altogether. We must be discerning. We must look for fruit. And we must seek wisdom from the Spirit, Scripture, and the counsel of mature believers.

Discernment in the ministry of deliverance

The ministry of deliverance — the act of confronting and casting out demons — was central to the work of Jesus and His disciples. It remains relevant today, but it must be approached with humility, discernment, and theological clarity. Not every problem is a demon. But some certainly are. And when they are, no substitute for spiritual authority will suffice.

In Luke 9: 1 we read where Jesus gave His disciples authority to drive out demons and that authority was certainly not limited to the first century as some have suggested.

Mark's Gospel records Jesus saying, "*These signs will accompany those who believe: In my name they will drive out demons.*" (16:17). While the authenticity of this longer ending of Mark is debated, the wider witness of Scripture and Church history supports the continuation of this ministry.

However, not all deliverance is biblical. Some practices border on superstition or manipulation. Others exalt the experience rather than the Lord. True deliverance ministry is marked by Christ-centeredness, Scripture saturation, prayerful dependence, and pastoral care. It is not a show. It is not a formula. It is a spiritual confrontation in the name and power of Jesus.

Deliverance should never be pursued in isolation from the local church. The local community of believers provides covering, accountability, and discernment. When someone is manifesting signs of spiritual bondage — whether unusual behaviour, intense spiritual resistance, or persistent torment — we must proceed with compassion, prayer, and a deep commitment to truth. The goal is not spectacle but freedom.

Furthermore, deliverance is not the end — it is the beginning. In Matthew 12:43–45, Jesus warned that when an impure spirit leaves a person, it may return with others if the house remains unoccupied. This is why discipleship must follow deliverance. The newly freed person must be filled with the Spirit, grounded in the Word, connected to the Church, and trained in obedience.

Discernment is essential. Some issues may look spiritual but have psychological or physiological roots. Other times, what appears natural is actually spiritual. This is why deliverance ministry must walk hand-in-hand with pastoral wisdom, medical insight, and prayerful community. The goal is not to chase demons, but to pursue wholeness in Christ.

In all things, we must remember that the name of Jesus is supreme. Demons tremble at His name. The power that raised Christ from the dead dwells in every believer (Romans 8:11). When we stand in that authority, we do not need to be afraid. We need only to be faithful.

The subtle strategies of demonic influence

While dramatic demonic manifestations grab attention in the Gospels, most of Satan's work in the world today is far more subtle. Evil spirits prefer to operate undetected, influencing thoughts, values, relationships, and systems in ways that undermine God's truth and enslave people to deception. As the Apostle Paul wrote, *"Satan himself masquerades as an angel of light"* (2 Corinthians 11:14). His greatest victories come not through terror but through lies that look like truth.

One of the key strategies of demonic influence is ideological deception. In 1 Timothy 4:1, Paul warns that *"the Spirit clearly says that in later times some will abandon the faith and follow deceiving spirits and things taught by demons."* False teaching is not merely human error; it can be spiritually inspired. Demons spread heresy by twisting Scripture, promoting half-truths, and exploiting human desires. Entire belief systems can be shaped by doctrines of demons.

This is particularly evident in movements that deny the divinity of Christ, the authority of Scripture, or the necessity of the cross. But deception can also take more respectable forms: the gospel of self-help, moralism without repentance, Christianity as nationalism, or spiritual practices divorced from biblical truth. When Christians embrace these distortions, they unwittingly partner with the enemy.

Emotional bondage is another method. Demonic oppression can fuel cycles of anxiety, bitterness, shame, rage, or despair. While not all emotional struggles are demonic in origin, the enemy often exploits unresolved wounds, lies we believe about ourselves or God, and generational patterns of sin. He whispers accusations and stokes fear, trying to immobilize believers through guilt or trauma.

Relational division also plays into the enemy's hands. Paul urged the Ephesians, *"In your anger do not sin: Do not let the sun go down while you are still angry, and do not give the devil a foothold."* (Ephesians 4:26–27).

Unforgiveness, gossip, pride, and conflict will all open doors for demonic influence. Satan thrives in disunity. He sows suspicion and offense, turning brothers and sisters against one another.

We must also be aware of strong cultural strongholds. These are systems of belief or practice that persist across time and geography, shaping societies in ways that oppose God. Paul refers to these as *"arguments and every pretension that sets itself up against the knowledge of God."* (2 Corinthians 10:5). Materialism, sexual immorality, racism, secularism, and occult practices often have demonic roots. They are more than sociological trends; they are spiritual battlegrounds.

To resist these subtle strategies, believers must cultivate spiritual discernment, immerse themselves in the Word of God, and walk in humility and accountability. The greatest defence against demonic lies is truth — not just abstract doctrine, but truth that is lived, loved, and proclaimed.

The role of demons in physical and mental health

Perhaps no area is more fraught with confusion and controversy than the relationship between demons and physical or mental illness. Historically, some Christians attributed nearly all affliction to demonic causes, while others, especially in the modern West, dismiss any spiritual involvement entirely. The truth is far more nuanced and must be approached with biblical clarity and pastoral wisdom.

The Gospels reveal to us that demons can, in some cases, cause physical illness. In Matthew 9:32–33, Jesus heals a man who was mute because of a demon. In Luke 13:11–16, a woman who had been bent over for eighteen years is described as having been crippled by *"a spirit."* Jesus calls her *"a daughter of Abraham, whom Satan has kept bound."* However, not all illness is demonic. Jesus also healed many who were sick without any reference to demons. The distinction is crucial. Misattributing every sickness to spiritual causes can lead to shame, false guilt, or rejection of needed medical care. At the same time, ignoring the potential spiritual dimension can prevent full healing.

Demons can also afflict the human mind. In Mark 5, the demon-possessed man lived in the tombs, cried out constantly, and harmed himself. His behaviour resembles certain psychological disorders. Yet when Jesus cast out the demons, the man was restored and found *"sitting there, dressed and in his right mind."* (Mark 5:15).

It is essential to avoid oversimplification. The human person is a very complex mix of spirit, soul, and body. Emotional trauma, neurological imbalance, chemical dysfunction, sin, and spiritual warfare often overlap. Discernment is needed. Sometimes what appears to be demonic may be medical. Other times, what seems purely psychological may have a spiritual root.

The church must embrace a holistic model of care. Deliverance ministry should never replace therapy, medical treatment, or pastoral counselling. Rather, it should be integrated whenever needed, approached with sensitivity, and bathed in prayer. Healing may come through medicine, through prayer, or both. The goal is not to diagnose demons, but to restore wholeness in Christ.

Pastors and ministry leaders should be trained to recognize when spiritual factors may be at play, while also being humble enough to refer to health professionals. Likewise, Christian counsellors and doctors should be open to the possibility of spiritual dynamics. We must work together, not in silos, as we care for hurting people. Above all, we must cultivate compassion. Those who suffer need safety, not suspicion. They need love, not labelling. Whether the affliction is demonic, emotional, or physical, our response must be the same: to bring the presence of Christ, the truth of the gospel, and the power of the Spirit into their pain.

Resisting the devil and taking back ground

The New Testament does not only describe the work of demons; it calls the Church to resist them. James 4:7 gives the template: *"Submit yourselves, then, to God. Resist the devil, and he will flee from you."* This is not passive spirituality.

It is active engagement. We are not told to fear the enemy, but to stand against him with confidence and authority. Resisting the devil begins with submission to God. Authority in the spiritual realm flows from relationship with the Lord. You cannot fight darkness if you are walking in it. Holiness is not just moral uprightness; it is spiritual power. The believer who walks in the light disarms the enemy.

The weapons of our warfare are not physical but spiritual. Paul outlines them in Ephesians 6:10–18: the belt of truth, the breastplate of righteousness, the gospel of peace, the shield of faith, the helmet of salvation, and the sword of the Spirit. These are not decorative metaphors. They are essential armour for spiritual survival. Truth exposes lies. Righteousness protects the heart. Whereas faith extinguishes the arrows of doubt and accusation. Salvation secures the mind. The Word of God is our offensive weapon. And prayer energizes the entire operation. Without these, we are spiritually exposed.

Taking back ground from the enemy will involve repentance, renunciation, and renewal. Where there has been sin, we confess. Where there has been agreement with lies, we renounce. Where there has been bondage, we invite the Holy Spirit to bring freedom. This is not a quick fix; it is often a process. But it is a powerful one.

We also take back ground by reclaiming territory in our lives, families, and communities which has been surrendered to darkness. That might mean removing occult objects, breaking unhealthy soul ties, ending toxic relationships, or changing the atmosphere of our homes through worship and Scripture.

Spiritual authority is not loud or showy. It flows from intimacy with Jesus. The seventy-two disciples returned with joy saying, *"Lord, even the demons submit to us in your name!"* (Luke 10:17). But Jesus replied, *"Do not rejoice that the spirits submit to you, but rejoice that your names are written in heaven."* (v. 20). Power is not the goal—relationship always is. And from that relationship flows everything we need to walk in freedom.

The demonic and the occult: doors best left shut

One of the most overlooked yet spiritually hazardous areas of demonic influence is the realm of the occult. Scripture is clear and unambiguous about God's prohibition of occult practices. In Deuteronomy 18:10–12, Moses warns Israel: *"Let no one be found among you who...practices divination or sorcery, interprets omens, engages in witchcraft, or casts spells, or who is a medium or spiritist or who consults the dead. Anyone who does these things is detestable to the Lord."*

These prohibitions are not arbitrary. They exist because occult practices are not neutral. They involve contact with spiritual powers outside the authority of God. Whether in the form of fortune-telling, astrology, tarot cards, séances, crystal healing, or spells, the occult opens doors to demonic influence. Even seemingly harmless or entertainment-based expressions of the occult can serve as entry points for spiritual bondage.

In the Western world, these practices often appear as recreational or cultural curiosities. But their roots and results are deeply spiritual. They offer forbidden knowledge and power, promising enlightenment or control. Yet behind their allure lies a dark reality: deception, dependency, and ultimately destruction. Demons gladly respond to human curiosity when it seeks power apart from God.

The book of Acts records how new believers in Ephesus responded when the gospel confronted their former way of life. *"Many of those who believed now came and openly confessed what they had done. A number who had practiced sorcery brought their scrolls together and burned them publicly."* (Acts 19:18–19). Their repentance was visible, costly, and complete.

Christians must be equally serious today. If occult practices have played any role whatsoever in our lives — whether through direct involvement, cultural background, or generational heritage — we must renounce them completely. That means confessing them before God, removing all associated objects or materials, and declaring Jesus as Lord over every area of our lives.

It also means being wise about entertainment and influence. Many movies, games, and books glorify the occult, subtly desensitizing us to its reality. We cannot be passive consumers of spiritual poison. We are called to holiness. To walk in freedom, we must shut the doors we once opened and guard our hearts from further intrusion.

Angels and demons: real or counterfeit?

Understanding the demonic requires a proper understanding of the spiritual world as a whole. Not all supernatural experiences are demonic. Scripture affirms the existence and ministry of holy angels, who serve God and His people. Hebrews 1:14 says, "*Are not all angels ministering spirits sent to serve those who will inherit salvation?*"

Angels are real, active, and often involved in human affairs. They deliver messages, protect the faithful, execute judgment, and carry out God's commands. Their presence in Scripture is not symbolic but tangible. They appeared to Abraham, Jacob, Daniel, Mary, and many others. In the early Church, angels opened prison doors and delivered apostolic guidance. However, where God sends truth, the enemy sends counterfeits. Demons can imitate spiritual experiences, giving false visions, dreams, or sensations meant to deceive. Paul warns in Galatians 1:8 that "*even if we or an angel from heaven should preach a gospel other than the one we preached to you, let them be under God's curse!*" Not all supernatural activity is from God.

This is why discernment is crucial. John commands: "*Do not believe every spirit, but test the spirits to see whether they are from God.*" (1 John 4:1). The test is not whether the experience feels powerful or positive, but whether it aligns with the Word of God and exalts Jesus Christ. Demonic spirits may masquerade as guides, ascended masters, or departed loved ones—but they always lead away from Christ, not toward Him.

In a spiritual culture hungry for experiences, Christians must be grounded in the authority of Scripture. Sensations, visions, and encounters must never become the basis of our faith.

The Word of God is our measuring rod. The Spirit of God will never contradict the Word He inspired. Angels serve under Christ's lordship. Demons rebel against it. When spiritual experiences arise, whether personally or in ministry, we must exercise prayerful testing. Is the message consistent with the gospel? Does it produce the fruit of the Spirit? Does it glorify Christ? If not, we must reject it and stand firm. Our confidence is not in the supernatural, but in the Saviour.

How then shall I live?

In light of the biblical reality of the demonic realm, how should we live as followers of Jesus? How can we avoid the traps of fear, denial, or unhealthy fascination? What posture protects us and equips us to walk in victory?

Stay rooted in God's Word. The Word of God is the plumb line for all spiritual experience and the sword of the Spirit in battle. When Jesus was tempted by Satan, He did not argue or negotiate. He responded with Scripture (Matthew 4:1–11). So must we. A believer who knows the Word walks in light, clarity, and confidence. Ignorance is dangerous; truth is power.

Keep in step with the Spirit. The Holy Spirit is our guide, our protector, and our source of discernment. He reveals the schemes of the enemy and empowers us to overcome. Galatians 5:16 urges, "Walk by the Spirit, and you will not gratify the desires of the flesh." Life in the Spirit is not mystical escapism—it is practical obedience and daily fellowship with God.

Live a life of repentance and holiness. Sin gives the enemy access. Holiness shuts the door. That does not mean perfection, but a heart which is continually turned toward God. Confession, accountability, and obedience are powerful weapons of warfare. Ephesians 4:27 says, "*Do not give the devil a foothold.*" Repentance removes his grip.

Cultivate a lifestyle of worship and prayer. Worship shifts the atmosphere. Prayer strengthens the soul. Together, they invite the presence of God and drive back darkness.

Paul instructs us to *"pray in the Spirit on all occasions with all kinds of prayers and requests."* (Ephesians 6:18). The praying and worshiping Church is the prevailing Church.

Renounce every agreement with darkness. Whether through past occult involvement, unforgiveness, bitterness, or rebellion, any area where we have agreed with the enemy must be broken. This is often a matter of deliberate prayer: *"In the name of Jesus, I renounce my involvement with _____ and declare Christ's lordship over every area of my life."* The enemy thrives in secrecy; he flees in the light.

Seek healing and deliverance where needed. Sometimes deep freedom comes through the prayers of others. James 5:16 says, "Confess your sins to each other and pray for each other so that you may be healed." Don't walk alone. If you sense persistent spiritual heaviness, fear, torment, or bondage, seek the counsel and prayer of trusted, mature believers.

Focus on Christ, not the demonic. Spiritual warfare is not about chasing demons. It is about walking closely with Jesus. When our eyes are fixed on Him, we are less likely to fall for the enemy's schemes. Hebrews 12:2 urges us to *"fix our eyes on Jesus, the pioneer and perfecter of faith."* The safest and strongest place to be is near the Shepherd.

We are not called to live in fear, but in faith. Not in confusion, but in truth. Not in bondage, but in freedom. The demonic realm is real, but it is subject to Christ. Colossians 1:13 tell us that have been transferred from the kingdom of darkness to the kingdom of light. We belong to the King. And His authority is now ours to exercise in His name.

So live alert. Live free. And live in the confidence that the Spirit who lives in you is greater than any spirit in the world.

5. JESUS AND THE DEFEAT OF SATAN: VICTORY AT THE CROSS

The cosmic battle: a war from the beginning

To understand the victory of Jesus Christ over Satan, we must first grasp the nature of the conflict. The Bible presents human history not simply as a chronological unfolding of events, but as a cosmic battle between the kingdom of God and the kingdom of darkness. This is not a war of equals, nor is the outcome in doubt. But it is a real war, with real casualties, waged in both the seen and unseen realms.

The roots of this battle trace all the way back before the creation of humanity. Scripture alludes to the fall of Satan, a created angel who sought to exalt himself above God (see Isaiah 14:12–15; Ezekiel 28:11–19). Though these passages address earthly kings, their imagery and language suggest a deeper spiritual reality — one in which a high-ranking angelic being rebels against his Creator. Revelation 12 offers a more direct account: *"There was war in heaven. Michael and his angels fought against the dragon, and the dragon and his angels fought back. But he was not strong enough, and they lost their place in heaven. The great dragon was hurled down — that ancient serpent called the devil, or Satan, who leads the whole world astray."*

From the moment of his fall, Satan has opposed the purposes of God. His hatred is particularly directed toward humanity, who bear the image of God. In the Garden of Eden, Satan (in the form of a serpent) deceived Adam and Eve, bringing sin, death, and separation into the world. This was not merely a moral failure; it was a hostile takeover. By aligning with the serpent, humanity surrendered its dominion and became enslaved to sin.

But even in that moment of defeat, God declared war. In Genesis God speaks to the serpent: *"I will put enmity between you and the woman, and between your offspring and hers; he will crush your head, and you will strike his heel."* (Genesis 3:15)

From that point forward, redemptive history is the unfolding of this promise. The seed of the woman would come. The serpent would be crushed.

This cosmic battle runs through the entire biblical narrative. Pharaoh's opposition to Moses was not merely political—it was spiritual. The idolatry of Canaan, the persecution of the prophets, the exile of Israel—all were expressions of the clash between light and darkness. The Old Testament closes with anticipation. The Messiah will come. The King will reign. And the enemy will be defeated.

Jesus' mission: not just to save, but to destroy

When Jesus arrives on the scene, His mission is often described in terms of love, grace, and reconciliation. And rightly so. He came to save sinners, to heal the broken, to proclaim the good news. But there is another side to His mission that must not be overlooked: Jesus came to destroy the works of the devil.

This is stated plainly in 1 John 3:8: "*The reason the Son of God appeared was to destroy the devil's work.*" This is a strong and violent verb. Jesus did not come to negotiate with evil, but to crush it. His entire life and ministry are acts of war. At His birth, Herod's violent reaction was more than political paranoia; it was demonic opposition. The incarnation was an invasion. Heaven broke into earth. God took on flesh, and hell trembled.

In His temptation in the wilderness (Matthew 4:1–11), Jesus confronts Satan directly. This was not simply a test of His obedience but a public declaration of authority. Where Adam failed in the garden, Jesus triumphed in the desert. Each temptation was met with the Word of God, and Satan was forced to flee.

Throughout His ministry, Jesus continually demonstrated His authority over demonic forces. In Mark 1:23–26, He drives out an impure spirit with a word, and the people are amazed: "*He even gives orders to impure spirits and they obey him!*" Time and again, demons recognize Him. They shriek, plead, and flee.

They know who He is and what He has come to do. The Gospels record over twenty distinct instances of Jesus delivering individuals from demonic bondage—each one a declaration of the inbreaking kingdom of God.

In Luke 11:20, Jesus says, "*If I drive out demons by the finger of God, then the kingdom of God has come upon you.*" This was not merely spiritual housekeeping. It was regime change. Every exorcism was a skirmish in a greater war. Satan's grip was loosening. His territory was being reclaimed.

Jesus also gave this authority to His disciples. In Luke 10:17, the seventy-two return with joy and report, "Lord, even the demons submit to us in your name!" Jesus responds, "I saw Satan fall like lightning from heaven." This was more than metaphor. Jesus was declaring that Satan's power was being dismantled. Not in full— not yet. But the end had begun. The kingdom of God was advancing. The strong man's house was being plundered. And the decisive battle was drawing near.

The cross: the unexpected victory

If we were to script the defeat of Satan, we might imagine a dramatic battle, a cosmic showdown of angelic armies. Instead, we are led to a wooden cross, outside a city wall, where the Son of God hangs between two criminals. To the watching world— and to Satan himself—it must have looked like defeat. But it was the greatest victory the universe has known. Colossians 2:13–15 declares, "*When you were dead in your sins... God made you alive with Christ. He forgave us all our sins, having cancelled the charge of our legal indebtedness, which stood against us and condemned us; he has taken it away, nailing it to the cross. And having disarmed the powers and authorities, he made a public spectacle of them, triumphing over them by the cross.*"

Here Paul reveals the spiritual dimension of the crucifixion. It was not merely a sacrifice for sin—though it was that. It was also a disarming of evil. The "*powers and authorities*" refer not only to human institutions, but to demonic forces. Jesus stripped them of their weapons. He exposed their powerlessness.

The cross, once a symbol of Roman brutality, became a banner of divine conquest. How did the cross accomplish this? First, by removing sin. Sin is Satan's greatest weapon. He accuses, condemns, and enslaves through guilt. But when Jesus bore our sin, He broke the enemy's claim. Romans 8:1 declares, *"There is now no condemnation for those who are in Christ Jesus."* Satan may accuse, but his charges cannot stick. The blood of Jesus silences him.

Second, by satisfying justice. The holiness of God demands judgment for sin. Satan exploits this, presenting God's justice as a barrier to mercy. But at the cross, justice and mercy meet. Jesus takes the penalty, upholding righteousness while offering forgiveness. The enemy's legal claim is nullified.

Third, by defeating death. Hebrews 2:14-15 says, *"Since the children have flesh and blood, he too shared in their humanity so that by his death he might break the power of him who holds the power of death — that is, the devil — and free those who all their lives were held in slavery by their fear of death."* The resurrection of Jesus was not just personal vindication; it was a cosmic overthrow. Death lost its sting. The grave lost its grip. The devil lost his throne.

The cross was not the end of Jesus' power over evil — it was the foundation of it. His resurrection confirmed the victory. His ascension sealed it. His enthronement declared it to all creation. *"And having disarmed the powers and authorities, he made a public spectacle of them, triumphing over them by the cross."*

The Resurrection and Ascension: Sealing the Victory

While the cross marked the decisive blow in the battle against Satan, it is the resurrection and ascension of Jesus that publicly declare and seal that victory. If Jesus had remained in the grave, the cross might be seen as a noble but tragic defeat. But the empty tomb changes everything. The resurrection is not just a miracle; it is a proclamation. In rising from the dead, Jesus triumphed over the final weapon of the enemy: death itself. Paul writes in 1 Corinthians 15:54-55, *"Death has been swallowed up in victory. Where, O death, is your victory? Where, O death, is your sting?"*

The resurrection declares that death is no longer the ultimate power. It has been dethroned by the risen King. Furthermore, Jesus' resurrection body is not a return to earthly life but a transformation. He is the *"first fruits of those who have fallen asleep"* (1 Corinthians 15:20). This means that His resurrection is not only proof of His own vindication but the guarantee of ours. If Christ has been raised, then those who belong to Him will also be raised. Satan's greatest threat has lost its power.

The ascension, often overlooked, is equally significant in Christ's triumph. In Ephesians 1:20–21, Paul says that God *"raised Christ from the dead and seated him at his right hand in the heavenly realms, far above all rule and authority, power and dominion."* Jesus is not just alive—He is enthroned. He reigns over every spiritual power, visible and invisible.

Hebrews 10:12–13 declares, *"When this priest had offered for all time one sacrifice for sins, he sat down at the right hand of God, and since that time he waits for his enemies to be made his footstool."* Sitting is the posture of completion and rule. The work is finished. The battle is won. The King is on the throne.

Satan has not yet been removed from the world, but he has been decisively defeated. His power is broken. His future is sealed. Revelation 20 makes clear that his ultimate end is the lake of fire, where he will be tormented forever. Until then, he rages against the church. But he does so as a defeated foe. This is why Christians can live with confidence and hope. We are not fighting for victory—we are fighting from victory. The battle is real, but the outcome is secure. Jesus has risen. Jesus reigns. And Jesus will return to complete what He began.

Christ's authority given to the church

The defeat of Satan by Christ is not a private victory. It is a shared one. The authority that Jesus exercised over demons, darkness, and death has been delegated to His church. This is a staggering truth. The same Jesus who silenced storms and cast out legions has given His followers the mandate to continue His mission.

In Matthew 28:18–20, the risen Christ says, "*All authority in heaven and on earth has been given to me. Therefore, go and make disciples of all nations... And surely I am with you always.*" The Great Commission is rooted in the authority of Christ. And that authority is now shared with His people.

Jesus promises in Luke 10:19, "*I have given you authority to trample on snakes and scorpions and to overcome all the power of the enemy; nothing will harm you.*" This is not a license for arrogance or spectacle, but a commission for victory. The church is not a hiding place; it is an outpost of the kingdom.

In Mark 16:17, Jesus declares, "*These signs will accompany those who believe: In my name they will drive out demons.*" In Acts, we see this lived out. Peter, Paul, Philip, and others exercise spiritual authority in the name of Jesus. They confront demonic powers, break chains of oppression, and establish the church in hostile territory.

But this authority is not automatic. It flows from relationship and obedience. In Acts 19, some Jewish exorcists attempt to invoke the name of Jesus without knowing Him. The demons respond, "*Jesus I know, and Paul I know about, but who are you?*" (Acts 19:15). The result is humiliation. The authority of Christ cannot be wielded like a magic wand. It is the fruit of union with Him.

This is why the armour of God in Ephesians 6 is so critical. Authority without integrity is very dangerous. Power without submission is futile. We walk in victory when we walk in truth, righteousness, faith, and prayer. The sword of the Spirit is only effective in the hands of those who are filled with the Spirit.

Moreover, spiritual authority is expressed in humility, not spectacle. Jesus washed feet. Paul suffered beatings. The apostles rejoiced in being counted worthy to suffer for the name. Victory in Christ is not about domination but about deliverance. It is not about control but about compassion. We carry the authority of Jesus to set captives free, not to exalt ourselves.

Living between D-Day and V-Day

Theologians have often compared Christ's victory over Satan to the events of World War II. On D-Day, the Allied forces landed on the beaches of Normandy. It was the decisive turning point of the war. From that moment, the outcome was sealed. Yet the fighting continued. The enemy did not surrender immediately. It was not until V-Day, several months later, that victory was fully realized.

So it is with the cross and the return of Christ. At the cross, Satan was defeated. At the return of Christ, he will be destroyed. In between, we live in the tension. The kingdom has come, but it is not yet complete. The enemy is defeated, but he is not yet silenced. This explains the paradox of the Christian life. We experience victory and struggle. We cast out demons yet battle temptation. We proclaim Christ's triumph, yet weep in spiritual warfare. The tension is real, but so is the power.

Revelation 12 offers a powerful picture of this reality. After describing Satan's defeat and expulsion, it says: "*They triumphed over him by the blood of the Lamb and by the word of their testimony; they did not love their lives so much as to shrink from death.*" (Revelation 12:11). Our victory flows from Christ's blood, is proclaimed through our testimony, and is sustained by our willingness to follow Him no matter the cost.

We do not wait passively for Christ's return. We live each day as overcomers. We pray, proclaim, resist, and endure. We advance the kingdom one life, one prayer, one act of love at a time. And we do so with joy, knowing that the outcome is already decided. We already know how this ends. "*The God of peace will soon crush Satan under your feet.*" (Romans 16:20)

The nature of Christian victory: present and future

Though Jesus has triumphed over Satan at the cross and secured ultimate victory through His resurrection and ascension, the daily experience of the Christian can still feel like a battlefield. Temptation persists. Spiritual oppression remains a reality.

Evil seems rampant in our world. This tension does not mean Christ's victory is incomplete, but that it is unfolding in time according to God's sovereign plan. Romans 8 describes this tension with remarkable clarity. Paul writes that all creation is groaning as it waits to be liberated from its bondage to decay (Romans 8:21–22). We, too, groan inwardly as we await our adoption and the redemption of our bodies. Though we have the first fruits of the Spirit, we still long for the fullness of salvation. This already-but-not-yet reality shapes how we engage in spiritual warfare.

Christ's victory is decisive, not partial. Satan is not an equal adversary who might still win. But like a cornered and desperate enemy, he lashes out against God's people. His power is permitted only within the limits God allows. Job's suffering makes this clear: Satan could only act within divine boundaries. The same is true today.

This is why we must hold fast to the truth that Christian victory is both positional and practical. Positionally, we are seated with Christ in the heavenly realms (Ephesians 2:6). We share in His authority. We are adopted, justified, and spiritually alive. Practically, we are called to stand, resist, pray, forgive, and endure. Victory is not simply declared — it is lived out in faith and obedience.

The weapons of our warfare

Because we live in a time when spiritual warfare is real, the New Testament provides us with clear instructions for how to fight. Ephesians 6:10–18 is the most detailed passage on the believer's spiritual armour. Each element of the armour is essential:

- *The belt of truth* secures everything else in place.
- *The breastplate of righteousness* protects our hearts from condemnation.
- *The gospel of peace* prepares us to move forward with confidence.

- *The shield of faith* extinguishes the flaming arrows of doubt, temptation, and fear.
- *The helmet of salvation* guards our minds with assurance.
- *The sword of the Spirit*, the Word of God, is our offensive weapon against deception.

Paul follows this description with a command to pray "*on all occasions with all kinds of prayers and requests.*" (v. 18). Prayer is not just a support activity—it is a primary strategy in warfare. It activates the armour and strengthens the soldier.

In 2 Corinthians 10:4–5, Paul reminds us that "*the weapons we fight with are not the weapons of the world. On the contrary, they have divine power to demolish strongholds.*" These strongholds are often rooted in false beliefs, addictions, pride, fear, and sin patterns. They are not merely behavioural issues but spiritual entrenchments. Through the Word, prayer, repentance, and community, they can be dismantled.

It is critical to note that the Church fights together, not alone. Paul uses plural language in Ephesians 6. The armour was not designed for a lone soldier but for an army. We stand shoulder to shoulder, praying for one another, encouraging one another, correcting one another, and advancing the kingdom together.

How then shall I live?

In light of Christ's decisive victory over Satan through the cross and resurrection, how should we live? How do we honour the triumph of our King in our daily walk?

Live from the finished work of Christ, not toward it. Many believers live as though victory is something to be achieved. But the gospel tells us that victory has already been won. We are not striving to earn acceptance or power; we are resting in what Jesus has already accomplished. Colossians 2:10 says, "*You have been given fullness in Christ, who is the head over every power and authority.*" To live from victory means we reject shame, fear, and performance-based religion. It means we stand confidently in Christ, knowing that our identity is secure and our enemy is defeated.

Resist the devil and renounce his lies. James 4:7 offers a simple but powerful formula: *"Submit yourselves, then, to God. Resist the devil, and he will flee from you."* Spiritual warfare is not about shouting or spectacle—it is about submission and resistance. When we submit to God's Word and will, we become impervious to the enemy's manipulation. Satan's most common strategy is deception. He is the father of lies (John 8:44). He tells us we are worthless, powerless, guilty, alone, unloved, or beyond hope. We recognize and reject these lies with the truth of God's Word. Like Jesus in the wilderness, we answer, *"It is written."*

Walk in holiness and obedience. There is no spiritual authority apart from moral integrity. When we live in wilful sin, we give the enemy a foothold. But when we walk in obedience—not perfection, but consistent, humble obedience—we walk in power. 1 Peter 5:8-9 urges us to be alert and sober-minded, because *"your enemy the devil prowls around like a roaring lion looking for someone to devour. Resist him, standing firm in the faith."* Holiness is our defence. Faithfulness is our strength.

Cultivate a lifestyle of worship and gratitude. Worship is warfare. When we exalt Christ, we dethrone idols and silence fear. Gratitude shifts our perspective from scarcity to abundance, from worry to trust. Paul and Silas sang hymns in prison—and the chains fell off. Worship reminds us that Jesus is King. It magnifies truth and minimises lies. It invites the presence of God and fortifies the soul. Whether alone or in community, worship is a daily declaration: Christ has won.

Advance the kingdom, don't just defend against darkness. Too often, spiritual warfare is reduced to defence. But Jesus called us to storm the gates of hell. We are commissioned to make disciples, proclaim the gospel, heal the sick, deliver the oppressed, and demonstrate the reign of God. Every act of love, justice, mercy, and truth is an act of war against the kingdom of darkness. We are not on the back foot. The enemy is. He is defeated. We are advancing. The Spirit of the Lord is upon us to proclaim good news to the poor, bind up the broken-hearted, and proclaim liberty to the captives (Isaiah 61:1).

Live in community, not isolation. Warfare is exhausting when fought alone. The enemy thrives in isolation but flees from unity. We need the body of Christ: for prayer, for accountability, encouragement, correction, and joy. Ecclesiastes 4:12 reminds us that *"a cord of three strands is not quickly broken."*

Engage deeply in the life of your local church. Be honest about your struggles. Pray with others. Celebrate victories. Bear one another's burdens. In doing so, we stand as one against the schemes of the enemy.

Fix your eyes on Jesus. At the heart of spiritual warfare is not demons or deliverance, but devotion. Hebrews 12:2 calls us to *"fix our eyes on Jesus, the pioneer and perfecter of faith."* Victory is not a technique. It is a person.

Look to the One who crushed the serpent's head. Trust the One who triumphed at the cross. Walk with the One who sends you in His name. The closer we are to Jesus, the less we fear the enemy. We do not overcome by formulas, but by faith in the Overcomer.

"They triumphed over him by the blood of the Lamb and by the word of their testimony." (Revelation 12:11)

6. SPIRITUAL WARFARE IN THE LIFE OF THE BELIEVER

Spiritual warfare is every believer's reality

One of the great misconceptions in the Church today is that spiritual warfare is a special concern for missionaries, pastors, or those who are particularly sensitive to spiritual realities. But Scripture makes it abundantly clear: every believer is engaged in a spiritual battle, whether they realize it or not. There is no opt-out clause. The moment we are born again into the kingdom of God, we are thrust into conflict with the kingdom of darkness.

Paul's words in Ephesians 6:12 are addressed to the entire church: *"Our struggle is not against flesh and blood, but against the rulers, against the authorities, against the powers of this dark world and against the spiritual forces of evil in the heavenly realms."* This is not just theoretical. It is not just poetic. It is real, personal, and unavoidable. The Greek word translated *"struggle"* in this verse refers to hand-to-hand combat. This is not distant warfare; it is intimate, intense, and constant. Paul is not warning of a potential future struggle but describing our present reality. Whether we feel it or not, the spiritual realm is active all around us, and we are participants in that conflict.

The Idea that a Christian can live a spiritually neutral life Is foreign to the New Testament. Jesus said, *"Whoever is not with me is against me."* (Matthew 12:30). There is no middle ground. We are either advancing the kingdom of God or resisting it. We are either walking in the Spirit or we are giving ground to the flesh. Spiritual warfare is not something we enter into just at certain moments — it is the context of our entire lives.

This war is fought not with worldly weapons, but with spiritual ones (2 Corinthians 10:4). It is waged not primarily against people, but against the lies, temptations, accusations, and schemes of Satan. And the battlefield is often the mind and the heart. What we believe, what we desire, and what we fear are not just psychological matters; they are spiritual territory.

The battle within: flesh vs. Spirit

While Satan and his demonic forces are external enemies, one of the most consistent themes in the New Testament is the internal battle between the flesh and the Spirit. Paul captures this struggle vividly in Galatians 5:17: *"For the flesh desires what is contrary to the Spirit, and the Spirit what is contrary to the flesh. They are in conflict with each other, so that you are not to do whatever you want."*

The *"flesh"* in this context refers not to our physical bodies but to our fallen human nature—our inherited tendency to rebel against God. Even though we have been made new in Christ, the remnants of the old nature still cling to us. Sanctification is the lifelong process of putting to death the deeds of the flesh and walking in step with the Spirit.

Romans 7 paints a raw and honest picture of this battle. Paul confesses, *"I do not understand what I do. For what I want to do I do not do, but what I hate I do... It is no longer I myself who do it, but it is sin living in me."* (Romans 7:15,17). Every believer can relate to this tension—the pull between what we know is right and what we are tempted to do.

This internal conflict is a key aspect of spiritual warfare. The devil capitalizes on the desires of the flesh. He tempts us with what already appeals to our fallen instincts. James 1:14 explains, *"Each person is tempted when they are dragged away by their own evil desire and enticed."* Satan does not need to create evil in us; he only needs to inflame what is already there.

But this is not a hopeless struggle. Paul does not end Romans 7 in despair. He cries out, *"Who will rescue me from this body that is subject to death? Thanks be to God, who delivers me through Jesus Christ our Lord!"* (Romans 7:24–25). There is victory, not by willpower, but by the Spirit. Romans 8 continues, *"Therefore, there is now no condemnation for those who are in Christ Jesus... because through Christ Jesus the law of the Spirit who gives life has set you free from the law of sin and death."* (Romans 8:1–2).

The battle is real, but the power of the Spirit is greater. Walking in the Spirit is not passive. It requires intentionality, discipline, and daily dependence. We must choose to set our minds on the things of the Spirit, to crucify the flesh with its passions, and to present our bodies as instruments of righteousness. This is warfare — not against others, but within ourselves.

Recognizing the enemy's schemes

Another vital element in spiritual warfare is the ability to discern the tactics of the enemy. Paul exhorts the Corinthians to forgive a repentant brother *"in order that Satan might not outwit us. For we are not unaware of his schemes."* (2 Corinthians 2:11). Many Christians today are unaware. We either ignore the enemy or give him too much credit. Both extremes are dangerous.

Satan's schemes are subtle and strategic. He is a liar (John 8:44), an accuser (Revelation 12:10), a tempter (Matthew 4:3), and a deceiver (2 Corinthians 11:14). His goal is not always to frighten us with obvious evil, but to mislead us with appealing distortions. Paul warns that *"Satan himself masquerades as an angel of light."* (2 Corinthians 11:14). He often wraps lies in partial truths.

One of his primary strategies is accusation. Even after our sins are forgiven, Satan loves to remind us of our failures. He whispers, *"God could never use someone like you. You're still dirty. You'll never be free."* These accusations aim to paralyze us with guilt and shame, even though Scripture assures us that there is no condemnation for those in Christ.

Another tactic is division. Satan will sow discord in families, friendships, and churches. Paul urges the Ephesian believers to *"make every effort to keep the unity of the Spirit through the bond of peace."* (Ephesians 4:3).

Disunity is not just a relational issue — it is a spiritual one. When believers turn on each other, the enemy wins. He also tempts us to compromise, just a little at a time. Rarely does spiritual downfall begin with overt rebellion.

It starts with small justifications: *"This isn't really sin. No one will know. I deserve this."* These thoughts chip away at our defences until the walls collapse. We must also be alert to spiritual passivity. When we disengage from prayer, Scripture, and fellowship, we become vulnerable. The enemy does not take days off. A complacent believer is an easy target. As Peter warns, *"Be alert and of sober mind. Your enemy the devil prowls around like a roaring lion looking for someone to devour."* (1 Peter 5:8).

Awareness of the enemy's schemes is not fear-driven paranoia. It is wise readiness. The call to be alert is a call to maturity. We stand firm not by our own strength, but by the armour of God and the victory of Christ.

Standing firm in the midst of resistance

A recurring theme throughout the New Testament is the call to stand firm. This language appears repeatedly in Paul's writings, especially in the context of spiritual warfare. In Ephesians 6:13, Paul writes, *"Therefore put on the full armour of God, so that when the day of evil comes, you may be able to stand your ground, and after you have done everything, to stand."* The emphasis here is not on attacking but on resisting and standing. This imagery suggests a kind of spiritual fortitude — an unwavering, immovable posture in the face of opposition. It calls to mind the soldier who refuses to retreat even when the battle is fierce. This is not passive resignation, but active endurance. We are called to take our stand not in our own strength, but in the power of the Lord.

Peter echoes this same idea: *"Resist him, standing firm in the faith, because you know that the family of believers throughout the world is undergoing the same kind of sufferings."* (1 Peter 5:9). Spiritual warfare is not an isolated or exceptional experience. It is part of the shared life of the Church. There is comfort in knowing that we are not alone.

To stand firm is to be deeply rooted in truth. It means we are not tossed back and forth by every wind of doctrine, every emotional swing, or every cultural pressure. We anchor ourselves in God's unchanging Word.

Psalm 1 describes the righteous person as "*a tree planted by streams of water,*" who bears fruit in season and does not wither under pressure. That is the posture of one who stands.

Standing firm also means cultivating spiritual endurance. In Hebrews 10:36, we are told, "*You need to persevere so that when you have done the will of God, you will receive what he has promised.*" Endurance is not glamorized in our culture, but it is essential in spiritual warfare. Very often, victory comes not by spectacular deliverance, but by patient perseverance.

The role of the mind in a spiritual battle

Perhaps the most strategic battleground in spiritual warfare is the mind. What we think, believe, imagine, and dwell upon shapes our spiritual vitality. Proverbs 23:7 says, "*As he thinks in his heart, so is he.*" Paul instructs the Romans, "*Do not conform to the pattern of this world, but be transformed by the renewing of your mind.*" (Romans 12:2).

Transformation begins with the mind. The enemy knows this and directs much of his attack at our thinking. He whispers lies about God, about ourselves, about others, and about our circumstances. These lies, if unchallenged, form strongholds — deep patterns of thought that resist the truth of the gospel.

Paul speaks directly to this in 2 Corinthians 10:5: "*We demolish arguments and every pretension that sets itself up against the knowledge of God, and we take captive every thought to make it obedient to Christ.*" This is the work of spiritual warfare: identifying lies, rejecting them, and replacing them with the truth. The lies we believe often masquerade as common sense or emotional logic. For example:

- "*God has abandoned me.*" (Lie)
- "*I'll never change.*" (Lie)
- "*I'm worthless.*" (Lie)
- "*This sin is too powerful to overcome.*" (Lie)
- "*God can't use someone like me.*" (Lie)

Each of these lies contradicts Scripture and must be exposed. The truth is that God never leaves us (Hebrews 13:5), transformation is possible (2 Corinthians 3:18), we are deeply valued (Matthew 10:29–31), sin has been defeated (Romans 6:14), and God delights in using weak vessels (2 Corinthians 12:9).

Renewing the mind is not a one-time event. It is a daily discipline. It involves soaking in the Word of God, meditating on His promises, and allowing His truth to shape our thinking. Philippians 4:8 urges us to think about what is true, noble, right, pure, lovely, admirable, excellent, and praiseworthy. This is not just good advice; it is spiritual strategy.

One practical tool in this battle is Scripture memorization. Jesus responded to Satan's temptations in the wilderness by quoting Scripture. The Word is our sword. When lies invade our thinking, having truth ready on our tongues can disarm the enemy and refocus our hearts.

Community as a fortress in the fight

Too many Christians try to fight spiritual battles in isolation. Whether from shame, pride, or misguided individualism, they suffer silently and wrestle alone. This is dangerous. God designed us to thrive in community, not just for encouragement and support, but as a strategic defence in spiritual warfare.

Hebrews 10:24–25 exhorts us, "*Let us consider how we may spur one another on toward love and good deeds, not giving up meeting together... but encouraging one another — and all the more as you see the Day approaching.*" The early Church understood this well. Acts 2:42–47 describes a vibrant community marked by shared life, worship, teaching, prayer, and generosity.

Community provides cover when we are weak, wisdom when we are confused, correction when we stray, and strength when we are weary. James 5:16 invites us to "*confess your sins to each other and pray for each other so that you may be healed.*" Healing and deliverance often flow through honest, humble relationships.

The enemy loves to isolate. He tells us no one will understand, no one else struggles like we do, and we are better off keeping things to ourselves. But isolation breeds deception. We need trusted brothers and sisters who will speak truth to us, pray with us, and remind us of who we are in Christ.

The Church is not just a support group. It is a spiritual army. When we gather in worship, we declare God's victory. When we pray together, we advance His kingdom. When we bear each other's burdens, we fulfil the law of Christ (Galatians 6:2).

Community also guards against spiritual pride. Left to ourselves, we can become either discouraged or arrogant. But in community, we are reminded of our need for grace, our dependence on others, and the power of collective faith. As Ecclesiastes 4:9–12 says, *"Two are better than one... Though one may be overpowered, two can defend themselves. A cord of three strands is not quickly broken."*

In the life of the believer, community is not an optional extra. It is essential. The battles we face are too intense and too strategic to fight alone. God has given us the Church as both a refuge and a weapon.

The armour of God: our daily defence

When Paul speaks about spiritual warfare in Ephesians 6, he does not leave believers unarmed. Instead, he paints a vivid picture of the armour of God—not a metaphorical idea but a spiritual reality. This armour is not meant to be admired from a distance or occasionally tested out; it is to be worn daily, prayerfully, and intentionally.

Paul urges, *"Put on the full armour of God, so that you can take your stand against the devil's schemes."* (Ephesians 6:11). This implies deliberate preparation. Just as a soldier does not enter battle without his gear, a Christian must not face the day without spiritual protection. Each piece of armour corresponds to a vital spiritual discipline:

- *The Belt of Truth:* Anchoring us in God's reality, not our emotions or the world's opinions.
- *The Breastplate of Righteousness:* Not our own, but Christ's righteousness imputed to us and lived out in moral integrity.
- *Feet Fitted with the Readiness of the Gospel of Peace:* Grounding us in the peace of Christ, prepared to stand and proclaim.
- *The Shield of Faith:* Protecting us from the flaming arrows of doubt, accusation, and temptation.
- *The Helmet of Salvation:* Guarding our minds with the assurance of who we are in Christ.
- *The Sword of the Spirit:* The only offensive weapon, which is the Word of God.

Paul concludes with the command, *"And pray in the Spirit on all occasions with all kinds of prayers and requests."* (Ephesians 6:18). Prayer is the context in which the armour is put on and used. Without prayer, the armour hangs on the rack.

This armour is not primarily defensive against people or circumstances, but also against spiritual deception and discouragement. Many battles are won or lost in the moment we believe truth or lies. The armour of God is not mystical; it is intensely practical. It shapes how we think, speak, act, and respond to pressure. It is God's provision for daily victory.

Victory through dependence, not strength

A critical correction to modern thinking about spiritual warfare is that it is not about summoning our own strength to conquer darkness. The gospel turns this on its head. Victory comes through surrender, not striving.

In 2 Corinthians 12:9, Jesus says to Paul, *"My grace is sufficient for you, for my power is made perfect in weakness."* Paul responds, *"Therefore I will boast all the more gladly about my weaknesses, so that Christ's power may rest on me."* This is the paradox of spiritual strength: we are strongest when we know we cannot win on our own.

Much modern teaching on spiritual warfare leans toward triumphalism—declaring victory, binding and loosing, and commanding in our own authority. While there is truth in standing in Christ's authority, we must remember that all our authority is derivative. We overcome not by our volume or boldness, but *"by the blood of the Lamb and the word of our testimony."* (Revelation 12:11). Humility is such a powerful weapon. James 4:7 says, *"Submit yourselves, then, to God. Resist the devil, and he will flee from you."* Submission precedes resistance. It is our union with Christ that makes us dangerous to the enemy. Apart from Him, we can do nothing (John 15:5).

This dependence is cultivated through spiritual disciplines: prayer, fasting, confession, fellowship, Scripture reading, worship, and silence. These are not mechanical rituals but means of grace through which we abide in Christ and remain spiritually alert. The Church has often confused noise with power. But true spiritual power is quiet, resolute, rooted in truth, and flowing from communion with God. Satan fears the humble believer who clings to Christ far more than the loud Christian who trusts in their own declarations.

Victory is not about constant triumphal feelings, but faithful obedience in weakness. It is refusing to quit, even when tempted. It is getting back up after falling. It is believing God's Word over our feelings. It is the daily death to self that opens the door to resurrection life.

How then shall I live?

Understanding spiritual warfare is not merely an academic or theological exercise. It demands a response. It must shape how we think, pray, speak, live, and relate to others. So, in light of the reality of the ongoing battle, how then shall we live?

Live aware but not afraid. Recognize that there is a real spiritual battle, but do not live in fear. Greater is He who is in you than he who is in the world (1 John 4:4). Awareness leads to vigilance, not anxiety. The cross of Christ has already secured the decisive victory.

Live rooted in the Word. Let Scripture be your compass, your nourishment, and your weapon. Read it daily. Memorize it. Meditate on it. Let it shape your thinking more than news cycles or social media. The Word is how you discern truth from lies.

Live prayerfully dependent. Do not try to fight spiritual battles in the flesh. Pray on all occasions. Pray alone. Pray with others. Pray the Scriptures. Prayer is your lifeline to the Commander of Heaven's armies.

Live in community. Surround yourself with fellow believers who speak truth, offer accountability, and bear burdens. Don't isolate. Let others pray with you and for you. Be the kind of friend who lifts up another's arms in battle.

Live humble and repentant. Keep short accounts with God. Confess sin quickly. Walk in humility. Satan gains ground where pride and unconfessed sin dwell. But he flees from the one who is hidden in Christ.

Live ready and dressed. Begin each day by acknowledging the armour of God which is already yours in Christ. Remind yourself of who you are in Christ. Anticipate opposition, but stand in the strength God has provided.

Live for the glory of God. Remember, spiritual warfare is not about personal power but about displaying the supremacy of Christ. Every act of obedience, every rejection of temptation, every word of truth spoken, every prayer whispered — these all declare that Jesus is Lord.

This is the life to which we are called: not one of fear or defeat, but of vigilant faith, rooted in grace, and empowered by the Spirit. The battle is fierce, but the victory is sure. Christ has overcome. And in Him, so shall we.

7. DELIVERANCE AND DISCERNMENT: A BIBLICAL PERSPECTIVE ON CASTING OUT DEMONS

Jesus and deliverance in the Gospels

One cannot read the Gospels without encountering the ministry of deliverance. Jesus didn't merely preach and heal—He confronted evil spirits directly and with authority. Casting out demons was not a fringe activity in His ministry; it was central to His demonstration of the Kingdom of God.

Mark 1:23–27 gives us this striking account:

"Just then a man in their synagogue who was possessed by an impure spirit cried out, 'What do you want with us, Jesus of Nazareth? Have you come to destroy us? I know who you are — the Holy One of God!' 'Be quiet!' said Jesus sternly. 'Come out of him!' The impure spirit shook the man violently and came out of him with a shriek."

This encounter, which took place in a synagogue—a religious setting—reminds us that spiritual oppression is not limited to pagan environments. Evil spirits can manifest even in places of worship. Jesus didn't hesitate or negotiate; He exercised divine authority and commanded the spirit to leave.

Throughout His ministry, Jesus cast out many demons. In Luke chapter 8, He frees a man possessed by a legion of demons—so many that they drove him to live among tombs, naked and tormented. Jesus restores him to his right mind.

In Matthew 12:28, Jesus says, *"If it is by the Spirit of God that I drive out demons, then the kingdom of God has come upon you."* His power over evil spirits was a sign of the inbreaking of God's rule.

Importantly, Jesus never sensationalized these events. He never built a show around deliverance. He was never distracted by demonic activity but dealt with it swiftly and decisively.

Note that His goal was always restoration—not spectacle.

Authority delegated to the disciples

Jesus not only delivered people from demonic power Himself; He empowered His followers to do the same. In Luke 9:1-2, *"When Jesus had called the Twelve together, he gave them power and authority to drive out all demons and to cure diseases, and he sent them out to proclaim the kingdom of God and to heal the sick."*

This was not a symbolic gesture. The disciples experienced firsthand the reality of spiritual conflict and the power of Jesus' name. When they returned, they joyfully reported, *"Lord, even the demons submit to us in your name."* (Luke 10:17). Jesus' response is both affirming and cautionary. He says, *"I saw Satan fall like lightning from heaven. I have given you authority... However, do not rejoice that the spirits submit to you, but rejoice that your names are written in heaven."* (Luke 10:18-20).

This statement reframes the entire discussion. The exercise of spiritual authority must always be grounded in relationship with God, not in power for power's sake. Our identity in Christ—not our ability to cast out demons—is our true foundation. Jesus warns us not to be enamoured with spiritual manifestations but to be anchored in salvation.

In Mark 16:17, Jesus promises that *"in my name they will drive out demons."* While this verse has textual complexities in some manuscripts, the testimony of the early Church confirms that this ministry continued beyond Jesus' earthly life. It was not limited to the apostolic age.

Deliverance in the early church

The Book of Acts reveals that the ministry of deliverance did not die with Jesus' ascension. In Acts 8, when Philip preached the gospel in Samaria, *"with shrieks, impure spirits came out of many."* (Acts 8:7). The power of the name of Jesus was still at work. In Acts 16:16-18, Paul casts a spirit of divination out of a slave girl in Philippi. She had been making money for her owners by predicting the future. Paul, *"troubled,"* finally commanded the spirit to come out in the name of Jesus—and it obeyed immediately.

This passage also illustrates that not all spiritual manifestations are from God. The girl's ability to predict the future may have seemed supernatural, but it was demonic in origin. The early Church had to practice discernment to distinguish between the Holy Spirit and unclean spirits.

Acts 19 presents another powerful scene in Ephesus, a city steeped in idolatry and occult practices. Paul's ministry was so effective that *"even handkerchiefs and aprons that had touched him were taken to the sick, and their illnesses were cured and the evil spirits left them."* (Acts 19:12). However, when some Jewish exorcists tried to invoke the name of Jesus without truly knowing Him, they were attacked by the possessed man and fled naked and wounded. The demon said, *"Jesus I know, and Paul I know about, but who are you?"* (Acts 19:15).

I am reminded of one of my encounters with a demon some years ago. I was leading a Home Bible Study group and one young man who attended had been struggling in his journey and I asked if he would allow me to pray for him. He agreed and we stood in this lounge room with a number of other people sitting around. I was a little concerned because I had felt there was some darkness in him and I was not sure what was about to happen. None of the people in that room had encountered the enemy up close before and I just had to trust God.

As I laid hands on the young man and prayed for God to touch him at his point of need, his face changed and he looked me in the eye and said with a slow, cold, aggressive voice, *"What are you doing? I know who you are and I don't want you to speak to me."* The people in the room were understandably shocked. This young man was normally very quiet, reserved and softly spoken.

I will spare you the details, but this encounter continued for a few minutes, and it was clear that the demon recognised the authority of Christ in me immediately and knew that he was about to lose a battle. The demon was cast out and the young man slumped back into the lounge and looked at me and said, *"What just happened?"* I simply said, *"God just set you free!"*

Spiritual authority is not a formula. It flows from genuine relationship with Christ. The name of Jesus is not some magic word—it is powerful because of the person behind it. Without faith and submission to Christ, the name holds no power in spiritual conflict. When I began to pray in Jesus' name over this young man – a cosmic battle which is raging across the universe, entered that lounge room in a way those people will never forget. Jesus is Lord and they got to see firsthand what that looks like!

Misconceptions and abuses in deliverance ministry

In many Christian circles today, the ministry of deliverance has become a source of controversy, confusion, and, at times, abuse. While the New Testament gives clear examples of deliverance, modern practice has often drifted from those moorings. On one hand, some deny the reality of demons altogether, reducing spiritual warfare to metaphor. On the other hand, others see a demon behind every sin, misfortune, or emotional struggle, and build elaborate rituals around deliverance that bear little resemblance to Scripture.

This imbalance leads to two major errors: demonic inflation and demonic denial. In demonic inflation, nearly every problem is attributed to a demon: anger, lust, depression, addiction, even minor inconveniences. This approach can foster fear, fatalism, and a victim mentality where believers blame the devil for every hardship or personal failure. It makes everything Satan's fault, bypassing the call to repentance, discipleship, and renewed thinking.

Conversely, demonic denial assumes that all such accounts were limited to biblical times or were merely misunderstood medical or psychological conditions. This view strips the spiritual realm of any practical relevance and leaves believers ill-equipped to deal with real spiritual oppression when it does manifest.

The New Testament presents a more balanced view. Not every sin is due to a demon, but demonic influence is real and active. Jesus didn't cast out demons from everyone, nor did He teach that every sickness had a demonic cause.

Paul, in his epistles, focuses far more on teaching, correction, and godly living than on direct confrontation with evil spirits. Yet he does acknowledge their presence and schemes (Ephesians 6:12). Discernment is therefore essential. Paul lists it among the spiritual gifts in 1 Corinthians 12:10: "*to another discerning of spirits.*" This gift helps distinguish what is of the Holy Spirit, what is of the flesh, and what may be from a demonic source. Without discernment, churches can fall into sensationalism or spiritual blindness.

The greatest safeguard against both extremes is Scripture itself. Any deliverance practice must be tested by the Word. Does it reflect the example and teaching of Jesus? Does it exalt Christ or the experience? Does it lead to freedom and holiness, or to dependency on a gifted individual?

Identifying demonic influence today

A common question among believers is how to recognize demonic influence in someone's life today. The New Testament shows us a variety of symptoms, but it does not offer a formula. What is clear is that demonic influence often mimics or exacerbates human brokenness, sin, and suffering. Some signs may include:

- Persistent patterns of destructive behaviour resistant to repentance
- Inexplicable torment, fear, or hatred of the things of God
- Supernatural strength or knowledge, as seen in the demoniac of Gadara (Mark 5)
- Occult involvement or generational bondage
- Physical manifestations without medical cause (though caution is needed here)

However, these indicators are not definitive. Mental illness, trauma, and sin can all produce similar symptoms. This is where wise pastoral care and prayerful discernment become essential. Jumping to conclusions without proper spiritual and emotional assessment can do harm.

In Mark 9, when Jesus confronts a boy with seizures caused by an unclean spirit, the disciples had previously failed to drive it out. Jesus explains that this kind *"can come out only by prayer."* (Mark 9:29). Not all deliverance is immediate or straightforward. It requires spiritual sensitivity, not bravado.

Another key principle is that demonic influence thrives in darkness. Exposure to light—through confession, worship, Scripture, and the presence of Spirit-filled believers—weakens its grip. Demons hate the truth and the name of Jesus. When believers walk in the light, fellowship with others, and bring hidden struggles into the open, the enemy's power is diminished.

Deliverance ministry, then, must be pastoral, not theatrical. It requires humility, not hype. It may involve quiet prayer, loving confrontation, Scripture reading, or fasting—but always in the context of a larger, broader process of discipleship and healing. Deliverance without discipleship is dangerous. Jesus warned that when a spirit leaves a person, it may return with others if the house is left empty (Matthew 12:43–45). The goal is not just removal of evil, but the filling of the Holy Spirit.

The role of faith and the name of Jesus

Central to all biblical deliverance is faith in Jesus Christ. Demons do not flee because of human charisma, eloquence, or emotion. They flee from the presence and authority of the risen Lord. James 2:19 says, *"You believe that there is one God. Good! Even the demons believe that—and shudder."*

What they fear is not religious talk, but the active authority of Jesus Christ in a believer who walks by faith. That is why the sons of Sceva in Acts 19 failed. They invoked the name of Jesus without submitting to His lordship. The power is not in the syllables of the name but in the reality of who He is and our union with Him. Faith activates that union. In Mark 16:17, Jesus says, *"These signs will accompany those who believe: In my name they will drive out demons."*

The authority to confront darkness flows from believing hearts aligned with God's will. This is not about shouting louder but about standing firmer.

Prayer plays a crucial role. Some deliverance comes instantly, while other situations require sustained prayer, fasting, and waiting on the Lord. The disciples learned this the hard way. When they failed to deliver a boy from torment, Jesus pointed to their lack of prayer (Mark 9:29).

The name of Jesus is not a mystical charm. It is the declaration of the One who triumphed over Satan through the cross. Colossians 2:15 says, *"Having disarmed the powers and authorities, he made a public spectacle of them, triumphing over them by the cross."* This is our confidence: Jesus has already won. Deliverance is not about gaining a victory, but enforcing the one Christ has already secured.

The Christian who knows who they are in Christ can stand boldly. When Satan accuses, we plead the blood. When he tempts, we resist with the Word. When he intimidates, we worship. When he lies, we speak truth. And when he oppresses, we invoke the name that is above every name.

The balance of authority and humility

In today's Christian landscape, one of the greatest dangers in the realm of deliverance ministry is spiritual arrogance. When a believer begins to see themselves as a "demon slayer" rather than a servant of Christ, the focus shifts from the glory of God to the performance of man. Jesus was never theatrical, never self-promoting, and never reckless in His encounters with demonic forces. His power was clothed in humility.

In Jude 9, we read an extraordinary statement: *"But Michael the archangel, when he disputed with the devil about the body of Moses, did not himself dare to condemn him for slander but said, 'The Lord rebuke you!'"* If even Michael, a mighty archangel, does not rebuke Satan on his own authority, how much more should we, as humans, approach spiritual warfare with reverence and caution?

This does not mean we cower or live in fear. It means we walk in dependent boldness, always pointing to Christ. We are not the deliverer—Jesus is. We are not the light—we bear the light. Our calling is not to be spiritual heroes, but faithful stewards of the authority Christ has given us.

Humility is not weakness. It is the posture that invites the power of God. When we pray, "Lord, deliver this person in Your name," we are not abdicating authority; we are exercising it rightly. We are acknowledging the Source while standing in the authority of His victory.

Freedom, restoration, and the whole gospel

Deliverance is never an end in itself. The goal is not just to expel evil but to restore wholeness and reestablish communion with God. Jesus came not merely to confront demons but to bring the fullness of salvation—forgiveness, healing, deliverance, and the indwelling presence of the Holy Spirit.

When someone is delivered, they need discipleship. They need Scripture. They need community. They need accountability. Jesus warned that a house swept clean can be re-occupied by more spirits if left empty (Matthew 12:43–45). Freedom must be followed by formation.

This is why deliverance should never be isolated from the broader life of the Church. It should occur within the context of pastoral care, biblical teaching, and spiritual support. The healthiest expressions of deliverance ministry are those embedded within churches that preach the gospel, disciple believers, and avoid sensationalism.

It is also important to remember that many forms of bondage are broken over time. A one-time prayer may be the beginning, not the end, of a person's journey to freedom. The renewing of the mind (Romans 12:2), the daily taking up of the cross (Luke 9:23), and the progressive healing of wounds all play a part in true deliverance.

The cross is the centre of it all. In His death and resurrection, Jesus disarmed the powers and triumphed over them. Deliverance is the application of that victory. It is not separate from the gospel; it is an extension of it.

How then shall I live?

In light of what we have now explored about deliverance and discernment, how then shall we live?

Live Christ-centred, not demon-focused. While we must not ignore the reality of the demonic, we must never fixate on it. Our focus should always be Jesus. He is our Deliverer, our strength, our peace. Talk more about Christ than about the enemy.

Live in the Light. Demonic influence thrives in secrecy, shame, and isolation. Bring your struggles into the open. Confess sin. Walk with others. Don't give the devil a foothold The more we walk in truth, the less power the enemy has over us.

Live discerning. Always Test every spirit. Not every supernatural experience is from God. Measure all things by the Word. Ask the Spirit for wisdom. Cultivate the gift of discernment through prayer, Scripture, and accountability.

Live prayerfully dependent. Deliverance is not a formula. It flows from intimacy with God. Build a prayerful life. Fast when led. Seek the Spirit's direction before confronting the demonic. Remain humble and submitted.

Live prepared to minister freedom. You may not be called to a formal deliverance ministry, but you are called to walk in the authority of Christ. Be ready to pray, to stand with others, to speak truth, and to resist darkness in Jesus' name.

Live with a pastoral heart. People are not just projects. Those experiencing oppression need compassion, patience, and care. Be quick to listen, slow to speak, and always seek restoration over display.

Live grounded in the gospel. Never separate deliverance from the message of the cross. Jesus' blood is our cleansing. His resurrection is our hope. His Spirit is our power. His Word is our sword.

The battle is real, but the victory is sure. We are not left alone or unequipped. The same Jesus who calmed storms, cast out demons, and raised the dead lives within us by His Spirit. Let us walk in that power, clothed in humility, grounded in truth, and anchored in love.

8. TESTING THE SPIRITS

The mandate to test the spirits

In 1 John 4:1, the apostle writes, "*Dear friends, do not believe every spirit, but test the spirits to see whether they are from God, because many false prophets have gone out into the world.*" This verse is not a suggestion. It is a command—a spiritual mandate for every believer living in a world filled with supernatural claims, religious experiences, and deceptive powers.

John was writing in a context where Gnostic heresies were infiltrating the church. False teachers were denying the incarnation of Christ while claiming deep spiritual insight. John's warning is clear: spiritual experiences, visions, and manifestations are not automatically from God. They must be tested. The supernatural realm is real, but not all supernatural realities are holy.

This is just as true today. We live in an age of spiritual hunger and unprecedented access to spiritual content—sermons, podcasts, dreams, books, prophecies, and YouTube testimonies. Some of these are genuine moves of God; others are deceiving spirits cloaked in Christian language. The Church must recover the biblical discipline of discernment.

To "*test the spirits*" means to evaluate the origin, content, and effect of spiritual influences. Are they from the Spirit of God, the spirit of man, or the demonic? Are they aligned with Scripture and the gospel of Christ? Do they promote truth, humility, holiness, and love—or pride, fear, confusion, and deception?

John continues in 1 John 4:2–3: "*This is how you can recognize the Spirit of God: Every spirit that acknowledges that Jesus Christ has come in the flesh is from God, but every spirit that does not acknowledge Jesus is not from God.*" This Christological test remains foundational. Any spirit or teaching that undermines the full humanity and deity of Christ is false. But discernment goes beyond doctrinal accuracy.

Paul tells the Thessalonians, "*Do not quench the Spirit. Do not treat prophecies with contempt but test them all; hold on to what is good, reject every kind of evil.*" (1 Thessalonians 5:19–22). Testing is not cynicism. It is spiritual maturity. We must remain open to the Spirit while guarding against deception.

The rise of spiritual counterfeits

Jesus Himself warned about false prophets and counterfeit signs. In Matthew 7:15–20, He says, "*Watch out for false prophets. They come to you in sheep's clothing, but inwardly they are ferocious wolves. By their fruit you will recognize them.*"

Fruit, not flash, is the test. A person may perform miracles or deliver stunning revelations and still be corrupt at the core. In Matthew 24:24, Jesus says, "*False messiahs and false prophets will appear and perform great signs and wonders to deceive, if possible, even the elect.*" Supernatural power does not automatically equate to divine endorsement. Pharaoh's magicians replicated Moses' miracles — for a time. The demonic realm has power, and it can imitate the gifts of God.

This is not a call to suspicion of all spiritual gifts. Rather, it is a call to discernment, rooted in the Word and empowered by the Spirit. In 2 Corinthians 11:14, Paul reminds us that "*Satan himself masquerades as an angel of light.*" Deception is most effective when it looks true. The devil's greatest tactic is not overt evil but subtle distortion. This is why emotional impact cannot be our guide. An encounter that feels powerful or deeply moving may not be of God. Many have been led astray by prophetic words that seemed accurate but ultimately bore bad fruit. Others have followed leaders with charisma but no character.

The Bereans in Acts 17:11 were praised because they "*examined the Scriptures every day to see if what Paul said was true.*" If they tested an apostle, surely we must test every teacher, every dream, every vision, and every supposed revelation today. God is not offended by our questions. He welcomes scrutiny when it is driven by a hunger for truth.

Discernment as a spiritual discipline

Discernment is not merely a momentary decision—it is a cultivated discipline. Hebrews 5:14 speaks of mature believers who *"by constant use have trained themselves to distinguish good from evil."* Like a muscle, discernment must be exercised. It begins with the renewing of the mind through Scripture. Romans 12:2 tells us, *"Do not conform to the pattern of this world, but be transformed by the renewing of your mind. Then you will be able to test and approve what God's will is."* The more we internalize God's truth, the more easily we recognize counterfeits.

Next, discernment grows in prayerful communion with the Holy Spirit. Jesus promised that the Spirit would guide us into all truth (John 16:13). As we abide in Christ, the Spirit trains our spiritual instincts. We learn to listen, to weigh, to wait, and to respond with wisdom.

Community is also vital. Proverbs 11:14 says, *"For lack of guidance a nation falls, but victory is won through many advisers."* Isolated believers are more vulnerable to deception. We need pastors, mentors, and trusted peers who can speak truth into our lives and confirm or challenge what we perceive spiritually.

Finally, discernment must be exercised with humility and love. It is not a weapon to destroy others, but a shield to protect the Church. It does not produce arrogance but reverence. When exercised rightly, discernment guards the flock, honours the Spirit, and glorifies Christ.

Weighing prophetic words and revelations

One of the most commonly misunderstood areas requiring discernment today is the realm of prophecy. In many Christian communities, prophetic words — words claimed to be from God, often spontaneous or visionary — are shared in public or personal contexts. These can be powerful and edifying when truly inspired by the Holy Spirit. The Apostle Paul encourages prophecy in 1 Corinthians 14:1: *"Follow the way of love and eagerly desire gifts of the Spirit, especially prophecy."*

Yet Paul also insists that prophecy must be tested. He writes, *"Do not treat prophecies with contempt but test them all; hold on to what is good."* (Thessalonians 5:20-21). This means we should not dismiss prophetic gifts out of fear of abuse, nor should we accept every word uncritically. The call is to balance openness with careful scrutiny.

1 Corinthians 14:29 further states, *"Two or three prophets should speak, and the others should weigh carefully what is said."* This communal weighing of prophecy protects the Church from manipulation, error, or even deception. A prophetic word must always be measured against Scripture, submitted to spiritual leadership, and tested by time and fruit.

A true prophetic word will exalt Christ, encourage holiness, and align with the revealed Word of God. It will not contradict Scripture, glorify the speaker, or manipulate the hearer. Even when a word is accurate, the spirit behind it matters. Prideful or controlling delivery can corrupt the fruit, even if the content is technically correct.

In the Old Testament, a false prophet was one who led people away from the Lord—even if their signs came true (Deuteronomy 13:1-3). God is more concerned with allegiance than with accuracy. The same principle applies today: a person may demonstrate insight, but if their character, theology, or fruit draws people away from truth, they are not speaking by the Spirit of God.

Distinguishing the Holy Spirit from a religious spirit

Another area requiring discernment is the difference between the Holy Spirit and what is sometimes called a religious spirit. While this term is not found in Scripture, it describes a counterfeit spirituality that mimics holiness but lacks true transformation and relationship with God. The Pharisees in Jesus' day were full of this spirit. They loved the appearance of godliness—long prayers, strict rules, public honour—but resisted the true work of the Spirit.

Jesus called them whitewashed tombs: clean on the outside but dead within (Matthew 23:27). In some churches today, the same pattern emerges. Performance-based righteousness, legalism, harsh judgment, and resistance to the move of the Spirit all reveal a religious mindset. This can masquerade as zeal for truth but is often a cover for fear, control, or pride.

The Holy Spirit brings conviction, but also comfort. He leads us to repentance, but also to intimacy. He produces fruit: love, joy, peace, patience, kindness, goodness, faithfulness, gentleness, and self-control (Galatians 5:22–23). When someone claims to speak for God but exudes arrogance, harshness, or fear, we must ask: Is this truly the Spirit of Christ?

Discernment helps us separate authentic spirituality from its counterfeits. It enables us to spot the difference between reverence and rigidity, between freedom and chaos, between true worship and emotionalism. Not all that is loud is anointed. Not all that is quiet is dead. The test is not the style—but the spirit.

1 Corinthians 12:3 gives a simple test: *"No one who is speaking by the Spirit of God says, 'Jesus be cursed,' and no one can say, 'Jesus is Lord,' except by the Holy Spirit."* True spiritual expression acknowledges Jesus' lordship—not just verbally, but in character and conduct.

Cultivating a discerning heart in a noisy world

We live in a world of overwhelming spiritual noise. Podcasts, books, sermons, dreams, prophecies, visions, Instagram reels, and YouTube testimonies flood our lives. Some of these are edifying; others are subtly destructive. The enemy does not need to lure us into blatant heresy—he only needs to distract, distort, or dilute the truth. To cultivate discernment, we must first slow down. Discernment requires time. In 1 John 4:6, John writes, *"We are from God, and whoever knows God listens to us; but whoever is not from God does not listen to us. This is how we recognize the Spirit of truth and the spirit of falsehood."* Listening—to God, to Scripture, to mature believers—is a prerequisite to recognizing truth.

Second, we must immerse ourselves in Scripture. Just as bank tellers are trained to recognize counterfeit money by handling the real thing, we become spiritually discerning by saturating ourselves in God's Word. The more we know His voice, the more easily we detect foreign ones.

Third, we must pursue intimacy with the Holy Spirit. Discernment is not just intellectual; it is relational. As we walk with God, He sharpens our perception. Colossians 2:3 says of Christ, "in whom are hidden all the treasures of wisdom and knowledge." To know Him is to gain insight.

Fourth, we must remain teachable. Proverbs 3:7 says, *"Do not be wise in your own eyes; fear the Lord and shun evil."* Arrogance blinds discernment. The truly discerning are the humbly dependent—those who know they need God's wisdom daily and seek it earnestly.

Lastly, we must surround ourselves with godly counsel. Even the most mature believer can misjudge spiritual matters. That's why Scripture consistently affirms the role of the community. Discernment grows in the soil of shared wisdom and tested truth.

Discerning in times of spiritual experience

In every generation, the Church has encountered seasons of revival, spiritual renewal, and outpourings of the Holy Spirit. These moments are often marked by passionate worship, supernatural manifestations, and an increased hunger for God. While these seasons can be beautiful and life-transforming, they are also susceptible to spiritual deception and emotional manipulation if discernment is not exercised.

The enemy is most active when the Spirit is moving powerfully. Where there is light, the counterfeit often creeps in unnoticed. In the wake of a genuine move of God, we often see excesses or false expressions that mimic the real. For this reason, discernment is never optional. It must accompany every spiritual high and emotional moment.

In the book of Acts, we see this dynamic clearly. In Acts 8, Philip is preaching in Samaria, performing miracles, and people are being saved. A man by the name of Simon, who had previously practiced sorcery, is baptized and follows Philip. Yet his motives soon prove impure—he tries to purchase the power of the Holy Spirit with money (Acts 8:18–21). Though he was drawn to the supernatural, he was still operating from the flesh.

This episode reminds us that spiritual hunger, even when sincere, must be anchored in truth. People can be swept up in powerful experiences while lacking true regeneration. That's why leaders must be watchful—not suspicious, but careful—shepherding spiritual movements with wisdom.

Paul speaks of this pastoral tension in 1 Corinthians 14. He encourages the exercise of spiritual gifts, especially prophecy, but insists they be conducted *"in a fitting and orderly way"* (v.40). God is not the author of confusion. Genuine spiritual activity will bear the marks of order, clarity, humility, and the exaltation of Christ.

Testing the spirits in everyday life

Testing the spirits is not only for extraordinary moments. It is for everyday decisions, relationships, and choices. The spiritual realm intersects with daily life more often than we realise. Ideas, worldviews, temptations, and even emotional responses may carry spiritual weight.

For example, consider a recurring thought pattern of despair or condemnation. Is that from God? Romans 8:1 tells us, "Therefore, there is now no condemnation for those who are in Christ Jesus." When thoughts arise that contradict God's Word, they must be tested and rejected.

When faced with major decisions—career moves, relationships, church involvement—we must discern: Is this leading me closer to Christ or drawing me away? Does it stir peace or confusion? Is it confirmed by Scripture and wise counsel?

Testing also applies to media, culture, and teaching. Many voices claim to speak truth, but only those rooted in Scripture and exalting Christ are worthy of trust. Paul urges Timothy to *"keep a close watch on yourself and on the teaching. Persist in this, for by so doing you will save both yourself and your hearers"* (1 Timothy 4:16).

We must become people who pause and pray. Who ask, *"Lord, is this from You?"* Who weigh every influence against the eternal plumbline of God's truth. This is not about paranoia. It is about spiritual maturity. Just as we grow in love, joy, and patience, we can grow in discernment.

How then shall I live?

Discernment is not a spiritual luxury. It is a necessity for every follower of Christ living in a world filled with spiritual noise and deceptive voices. So how then shall we live?

Live rooted in Scripture. The Word of God is our measuring rod. If you want to grow in discernment, read, meditate on, and memorise Scripture. Know the real, and you will detect the counterfeit. Let the Word dwell richly in you (Colossians 3:16).

Live in step with the Holy Spirit. Walk daily with the Spirit, seeking His voice, sensitivity, and counsel. He is the Spirit of truth. As we yield to Him, He refines our spiritual instincts and alerts us to deception. Don't grieve Him — walk with Him.

Live in community. Submit your experiences, revelations, and decisions to trusted leaders and fellow believers. Don't isolate. We discern better together. Iron sharpens iron, and protection is found in the wisdom of the faithful.

Live humble and teachable. A discerning spirit is a humble spirit. Be willing to admit when you've misjudged something. Receive correction. Stay teachable. Pride blinds, but humility sees clearly.

Live courageously. Discernment sometimes means standing against popular opinion. It may mean speaking out against error or leaving a toxic influence. Don't be afraid. The Spirit of God gives boldness and peace.

Live Anchored in Christ. Let Jesus be the centre of your theology, your spirituality, your affections. Test everything by Him. Does it glorify Christ? Does it lead to holiness and love? He is the truth. Abide in Him.

As the world grows darker and spiritual confusion increases, the people of God must shine brighter—not just with passion, but with discernment. We must be wise as serpents and innocent as doves. We must be people of the Word and the Spirit, of truth and grace. And above all, we must be people who know their Shepherd's voice and follow Him alone.

9. STANDING FIRM IN THE BATTLE

Strengthened in the Lord, not in ourselves

Paul's well-known exhortation in Ephesians 6:10–18 begins with this vital command: *"Finally, be strong in the Lord and in his mighty power."* Before he even mentions the armour, Paul grounds the believer's strength not in personal willpower, knowledge, or experience, but in the Lord Himself. This is foundational. Spiritual warfare is not a battle of equals—Satan is a created being, and God is the omnipotent Creator. The believer's confidence is not found in self, but in union with Christ.

The command to *"be strong"* is not a call to summon inner strength, but to rely on an external, divine source. The phrase *"in the Lord"* echoes throughout Paul's letters as shorthand for the believer's new identity. We are not standing alone. We are hidden with Christ in God (Colossians 3:3). We are seated with Him in heavenly places (Ephesians 2:6). We fight from victory, not for victory.

The phrase *"His mighty power"* recalls the same power Paul referenced in Ephesians 1:19–20—*"his incomparably great power for us who believe. That power is the same as the mighty strength he exerted when he raised Christ from the dead."* The resurrection power that defeated sin and death is the same power that fortifies us in spiritual battle. This is essential, because the reality of spiritual warfare is not a metaphor—it is a lived experience. We are engaged in conflict with invisible, intelligent, and malevolent spiritual beings. Without the strength and protection of God, we would be overwhelmed. But with Him, we are more than conquerors.

Understanding the nature of the battle

Paul continues in Ephesians 6:11–12: *"Put on the full armour of God, so that you can take your stand against the devil's schemes. For our struggle is not against flesh and blood, but against the rulers, against the authorities, against the powers of this dark world and against the spiritual forces of evil in the heavenly realms."*

Here Paul outlines both the strategy and the scope of the battle. First, he urges believers to *"put on the full armour of God."* This armour is not optional. We cannot pick and choose which pieces we feel comfortable wearing. The implication is that without this armour, we are vulnerable to the enemy's attacks.

The reason for this armour is *"so that you can take your stand against the devil's schemes."* The enemy is not disorganized or reckless. He operates with cunning, strategy, and persistence. The Greek word for *"schemes"* (*methodeia*) suggests methodical deception and ambush. Satan uses lies, temptations, accusations, distractions, distortions, and spiritual oppression to undermine believers.

Importantly, Paul emphasizes that our struggle is *"not against flesh and blood."* Humans are not the real enemy. The anger, betrayal, persecution, or injustice we experience from others is often fuelled by spiritual influences. When we demonize people, we lose sight of the real enemy. When we remember that the true battle is spiritual, we fight with spiritual weapons — prayer, truth, forgiveness, and faith.

The scope of the battle is sobering. Paul lists four tiers of demonic hierarchy — rulers, authorities, powers, and spiritual forces of evil. This suggests an organized network of demonic beings influencing systems, cultures, and individuals. This is not to create paranoia, but to cultivate awareness. The enemy is real, but he is defeated. Christ has already triumphed over these powers through the cross (Colossians 2:15). Our task is not to defeat them again, but to stand in Christ's finished victory.

The call to stand firm

Three times in Ephesians 6:11–14, Paul uses the phrase *"stand."* This repetition is significant. The battle posture for the believer is not running, hiding, or even chasing the enemy — it is standing firm. *"Stand firm then, with the belt of truth buckled around your waist..."* (Ephesians 6:14). This is the posture of a soldier who is grounded, immovable, and prepared.

In Roman military context, to stand was to hold your assigned position. Retreat was not an option. Soldiers were trained to hold the line. In spiritual warfare, standing firm means refusing to yield to lies, temptation, fear, or doubt. It means holding to truth when everything around us shifts. It means maintaining peace when conflict erupts. It means trusting God when circumstances scream otherwise.

Paul's use of *"stand"* also echoes Exodus 14:13, where Moses tells the Israelites as they face the Red Sea, *"Do not be afraid. Stand firm and you will see the deliverance the Lord will bring you today."* In other words, victory is God's work. Our role is to trust, obey, and remain grounded.

Standing firm is not passive. It is an active resistance. James 4:7 says, *"Submit yourselves, then, to God. Resist the devil, and he will flee from you."* The enemy cannot withstand a believer who is fully submitted to God, clothed in His armour, and standing on His promises.

The belt of truth and the breastplate of righteousness

Paul begins listing the armour of God with these words in Ephesians 6:14: *"Stand firm then, with the belt of truth buckled around your waist, with the breastplate of righteousness in place."* These two foundational pieces are vital to every believer's readiness.

The belt of truth is the first piece mentioned, not by accident. In ancient Roman armour, the belt secured the tunic and held the sword. Without it, a soldier's garments would greatly hinder his movement. Spiritually, truth is what holds everything together. Jesus prayed in John 17:17, *"Sanctify them by the truth; your word is truth."*

Truth is not just facts — it is the unchanging, revealed Word of God. To fasten the belt of truth is to reject lies and deception, to renew our minds with Scripture, and to ground our identity in who God says we are. Truth keeps us from being tossed by every wind of doctrine or cultural opinion.

The breastplate of righteousness protects the heart. In battle, a strike to the chest could be fatal. Spiritually, our "heart" is the centre of affections, motivations, and will. Righteousness protects this vital area. This is not our own righteousness, but Christ's. Paul says in Philippians 3:9 that he wants to *"be found in him, not having a righteousness of my own… but that which is through faith in Christ."* To wear the breastplate is to rest in the finished work of Jesus, knowing we are justified, forgiven, and accepted.

But righteousness also speaks of right living. The believer who walks in obedience and holiness is protected from many of the enemy's attacks. Unconfessed sin opens doors to spiritual oppression. The enemy delights in accusing, but when we walk uprightly, we silence his voice.

The gospel of peace and the shield of faith

Ephesians 6:15–16 continues, *"and with your feet fitted with the readiness that comes from the gospel of peace. In addition to all this, take up the shield of faith, with which you can extinguish all the flaming arrows of the evil one."*

Roman soldiers wore sandals with spikes on the soles to provide stability in combat. These allowed them to hold their ground and move swiftly. Paul compares this to the readiness given by the gospel of peace. Peace with God, through Christ, is what steadies our steps.

Romans 5:1 tells us, *"Therefore, since we have been justified through faith, we have peace with God through our Lord Jesus Christ."* This peace gives us assurance in battle. We do not fight for approval but from a place of reconciliation.

Moreover, the gospel itself makes us ready to move. Isaiah 52:7 declares, *"How beautiful on the mountains are the feet of those who bring good news."* A believer grounded in peace is also eager to proclaim that peace to others. Spiritual warfare is not only defensive — it includes advancing the Kingdom.

The shield of faith was a large, door-shaped shield designed to cover the whole body. Roman shields were often soaked in water before battle to extinguish flaming arrows. Paul says that faith does exactly that — it quenches the fiery darts of the evil one.

These flaming arrows will usually include doubts, temptations, accusations, fear, and lies. Faith is not blind optimism; it is confident trust in the character and promises of God. Hebrews defines faith as *"confidence in what we hope for and assurance about what we do not see."* (11:1). When Satan hurls fiery lies — *"God has abandoned you," "You're a failure," "This will never change"* – faith lifts the shield and says, "But God said..." It is not the strength of our faith that saves us, but the object of our faith. Even a mustard seed of true faith, directed toward the sovereign Lord, is enough to silence the enemy.

The helmet of salvation and the sword of the Spirit

Paul writes in Ephesians 6:17, *"Take the helmet of salvation and the sword of the Spirit, which is the word of God."* These final two pieces complete the armour — and both are essential for the mind and for active engagement.

The helmet of salvation protects the mind. In battle, a head injury is often fatal. Spiritually, the mind is the battlefield. Thoughts of despair, defeat, or deception are how the enemy often attacks. The helmet reminds us of our secure position in Christ. Salvation is not merely a past event or future hope — it is a present reality.

In 1 Thessalonians 5:8, Paul calls it *"the hope of salvation as a helmet."* When we remember that we are saved, being saved, and will be saved, our minds are shielded from fear and discouragement.

The sword of the Spirit is the only offensive weapon in the armour. It is "the word of God" — both the written Scriptures and the spoken word (rhema) applied in the moment. Jesus modelled this in Matthew 4, when He was tempted by Satan in the wilderness. Three times, He responded, *"It is written,"* and quoted Scripture.

The sword is not to be wielded recklessly. It requires training and humility. Hebrews 4:12 says the Word is *"sharper than any double-edged sword... it judges the thoughts and attitudes of the heart."* It pierces, but it also heals. It convicts, but it also comforts.

The believer who knows the Word, meditates on it, and speaks it with authority can cut through lies, confusion, and demonic interference. But this sword must be used under the Spirit's direction—not to win arguments, but to reveal truth and bring freedom.

Prayer: the power that activates the armour

Paul concludes his teaching on the armour of God with these words: *"And pray in the Spirit on all occasions with all kinds of prayers and requests. With this in mind, be alert and always keep on praying for all the Lord's people."* (Ephesians 6:18). This verse is not a separate thought—it is the essential power source for all the armour. Without prayer, the armour remains theoretical.

Prayer is the means by which we stay connected to the source of our strength. It is through prayer that truth is internalized, faith is renewed, righteousness is applied, and the Word is wielded.

Paul calls us to pray *"in the Spirit."* This means more than just praying fervently or emotionally—it means aligning our prayers with the will of God as led by the Holy Spirit. Romans 8:26-27 reminds us that the Spirit helps us in our weakness and intercedes for us according to God's will.

Paul also emphasizes the variety and frequency of prayer: *"on all occasions with all kinds of prayers and requests."* Spiritual warfare requires constant communication with God—prayers of thanksgiving, intercession, confession, and petition. There is no formula—only communion.

Moreover, Paul urges alertness and persistence in prayer. Spiritual battle is ongoing, and the enemy never sleeps. That's why Paul says, *"Be alert."* A soldier who falls asleep on duty endangers the whole unit. Likewise, a Christian who ceases to pray becomes vulnerable.

Prayer is also intercessory — *"always keep on praying for all the Lord's people."* We are not in this battle alone. We fight as a body. We are to uphold one another, stand in the gap, and contend for the saints. The armour of God was never meant to be worn in isolation — it is for the Church, the army of God, united in faith.

The warfare mindset: a call to readiness

Living with a warfare mindset does not mean living in fear, paranoia, or a demon-behind-every-bush mentality. It means being spiritually awake, discerning, and ready. Peter writes, *"Be alert and of sober mind. Your enemy the devil prowls around like a roaring lion looking for someone to devour. Resist him, standing firm in the faith..."* (1 Peter 5:8-9). To be alert is to be spiritually aware — to recognize when the enemy is at work and to resist him with faith, truth, and prayer.

Jesus lived with this mindset. He was never surprised by the schemes of the enemy. In the wilderness, He stood firm with the Word. In the Garden, He prayed fervently. On the cross, He triumphed through surrender. His entire ministry was one of victory over darkness. And He has called us to walk as He did.

A warfare mindset is also a Kingdom mindset. It remembers that this world is not our home. We are engaged in a cosmic battle for souls, for truth, for righteousness. It's not about political victory or personal comfort — it's about advancing the reign of Christ through love, truth, and sacrifice.

This mindset affects how we pray, how we worship, how we make decisions. It keeps us from spiritual complacency. It reminds us that the enemy is defeated, but still active. It calls us to vigilance, not panic; to boldness, not bravado.

How then shall I live?

The armour of God is not a concept to be admired — it is a reality to be lived. It is God's provision for daily, victorious Christian living. So how then shall we live?

Live armoured daily. The armour is not ceremonial or symbolic. It is practical and necessary. Begin each day with intentional awareness: Lord, clothe me with truth, righteousness, peace, faith, salvation, and the Word. Don't leave the house spiritually undressed.

Live dependent on God's strength. Spiritual warfare is not about your strength, willpower, or strategy. It is about abiding in Christ and walking in His power. Be strong in the Lord, not in yourself. Stay close to the source.

Live alert and discerning. Pay attention. Is that discouragement from the Lord? Is that temptation a trap? Is that conflict about more than meets the eye? Ask the Spirit to heighten your spiritual senses.

Live grounded in Scripture. The Word of God is your sword. Read it, speak it, memorize it, live it. Let the truth sanctify your mind and expose the enemy's lies. You don't need a new revelation — you need to stand on the eternal one.

Live Prayerfully. Without prayer, the armour has no power. Pray at all times — in the car, at work, before decisions, in moments of fear or temptation. Talk to your Commander. Draw strength from Him.

Live with Eternal Purpose. Remember why the battle matters. Souls are at stake. Truth is worth defending. Holiness is worth pursuing. Christ is worth everything. Keep your eyes on the prize.

The armour of God is not heavy — it is liberating. It frees us from fear, from deception, from defeat. It empowers us to stand when everything shakes. And it reminds us that we are not fighting for victory — we are fighting from it. So, stand. Stand firm in the Lord. Stand clothed in His truth. Stand with your feet planted in peace. Lift your shield. Draw your sword. Pray without ceasing. And when the battle rages, and the dust settles — you will still be standing.

10. VICTORY THROUGH THE CROSS: CHRIST'S TRIUMPH OVER DARKNESS

The cross was a cosmic confrontation

The crucifixion of Jesus Christ was not merely a political or religious execution—it was a cosmic confrontation. At the heart of the cross lies a supernatural battle between good and evil, light and darkness, truth and deception. The stakes were not just temporal, but eternal. When Jesus was nailed to that Roman cross, the unseen realm trembled.

The apostle Paul writes in Colossians 2:13-15:

"When you were dead in your sins and in the uncircumcision of your flesh, God made you alive with Christ. He forgave us all our sins, having cancelled the charge of our legal indebtedness, which stood against us and condemned us; he has taken it away, nailing it to the cross. And having disarmed the powers and authorities, he made a public spectacle of them, triumphing over them by the cross."

These verses reveal two simultaneous victories achieved through the cross: one in the realm of human redemption and the other in the spiritual realm of demonic resistance. On one hand, Jesus bore the full weight of our sin, satisfying divine justice and granting forgiveness. On the other, He stripped demonic powers of their authority and shamed them publicly.

The cross was not Satan's moment of triumph—it was his undoing. What looked like defeat was, in fact, the decisive victory. Jesus Himself had foretold this when He said, *"Now is the time for judgment on this world; now the prince of this world will be driven out."* (John 12:31).

The cross was not just about substitution—it was also about confrontation. It was the fulfilment of the first messianic prophecy in Genesis 3:15, where God says to the serpent, *"He will crush your head, and you will strike his heel."* On the cross, the serpent bruised the heel of Christ, but Christ crushed his head.

Disarming the powers and authorities

Paul's language in Colossians 2:15 is striking. He says that Christ *"disarmed the powers and authorities."* These terms refer to demonic hierarchies — fallen angels, principalities, and spiritual forces of evil. The Greek word for *"disarmed"* (*apekduomai*) means to strip away weapons or remove garments, leaving one exposed and vulnerable.

At the cross, Jesus stripped away the weaponry of the enemy. He removed their right to accuse, to condemn, and to hold humanity in bondage. This was no partial victory — it was comprehensive. The law, which had empowered sin and provided the legal basis for accusation, was satisfied in Christ.

In Revelation 12:10, a loud voice in heaven proclaims, *"Now have come the salvation and the power and the kingdom of our God, and the authority of his Messiah. For the accuser of our brothers and sisters, who accuses them before our God day and night, has been hurled down."* The cross rendered Satan's courtroom powerless.

Furthermore, Paul says Jesus *"made a public spectacle of them."* This phrase evokes the image of an ancient Roman triumphal procession — where a conquering general would parade his defeated enemies through the city as a demonstration of power. Christ did not win quietly. His victory was cosmic, visible to angels and demons alike. Though the world saw a broken man on a cross, the heavens saw a conquering King.

This imagery would have resonated deeply with Paul's audience in the Roman Empire. They knew the meaning of triumph. Christ's cross was not an embarrassment — it was a throne. His crucifixion was not a setback — it was an enthronement.

To live in the power of this reality is to understand that we are not striving for victory — we are standing in it. The demonic powers have been exposed. Their lies have been unmasked. Their weapons have been seized. The believer's task is not to fight a new war, but to enforce the outcome of a war already won.

Transferring authority to the church

Jesus did not keep His victory to Himself. He delegated it. Before His ascension, He declared, *"All authority in heaven and on earth has been given to me. Therefore go..."* (Matthew 28:18-19). The Great Commission begins with a declaration of total authority. This is the foundation of mission, evangelism, and spiritual warfare.

Christ's triumph over darkness was not merely a private or spiritual matter—it had implications for the entire world. Through His death and resurrection, He broke the power of sin, conquered death, and defeated Satan. Then He gave His Church the keys of the Kingdom (Matthew 16:19).

In Luke 10:19, Jesus says to His disciples, *"I have given you authority to trample on snakes and scorpions and to overcome all the power of the enemy; nothing will harm you."* This is not an invitation to recklessness or showmanship. It is a reminder that the believer's authority is rooted in Christ's finished work.

The early Church understood this. In Acts, we see believers casting out demons, healing the sick, and proclaiming the gospel boldly. They were not superstitious or obsessed with demons, but they were aware of the spiritual battle and confident in Christ's authority.

Yet, it's crucial to remember that this authority flows from submission. James 4:7 says, *"Submit yourselves, then, to God. Resist the devil, and he will flee from you."* Authority without submission leads to pride and presumption. But authority under Christ's Lordship leads to victory.

To operate in this delegated authority is to walk in alignment with Jesus' mission. It means we confront darkness—not just in overt spiritual manifestations, but in injustice, deception, addiction, and despair. Every place where the enemy has laid claim, the Church is called to reclaim in Jesus' name. This transfer of authority also means we are no longer victims.

Though we may suffer, we are not overcome. Though we are attacked, we are not abandoned. The cross was not just Christ's triumph—it is ours. We are co-heirs with Him (Romans 8:17). We are more than conquerors (Romans 8:37). We are the Church against which the gates of hell will not prevail (Matthew 16:18).

The enemy's ongoing strategies

Even though Satan has been disarmed and defeated by the cross, he continues to wage war using deception, accusation, and intimidation. His power has been broken, but his influence remains in the world. His strategy now is not to win, but to distract, divide, and disempower those who belong to Christ.

Jesus described the devil as *"a liar and the father of lies"* (John 8:44). He masquerades as an angel of light, disguising his attacks with false doctrine, prideful ambition, or seductive compromise. He aims to sow confusion, fear, legalism, and unbelief in the hearts of believers. Revelation 12:10 calls him *"the accuser of our brothers and sisters,"* who accuses them before God day and night. Though Christ has silenced those accusations with His blood, many believers still live under the weight of shame, doubt, or spiritual insecurity. Satan whispers, *"You're not really forgiven… God can't use you… You'll never change."*

His goal is not to overpower us by force—he cannot—but to tempt us to surrender territory Christ has already claimed. He wants us to live as if the cross didn't happen, as if the victory were still in question. His strategies only succeed when we forget who we are and whose we are. Paul reminds the Corinthians that *"we are not unaware of his schemes."* (2 Corinthians 2:11). The early Church lived in alertness, not paranoia. They knew the enemy was real, but they also knew he was defeated. They resisted him, not with fear, but with faith.

Spiritual warfare in the post-resurrection era is not about fighting for victory—it is about enforcing it. The believer's posture is not defensive retreat but confident advance. We are not called to tremble in the shadows but to walk in the light.

The church as the visible expression of Christ's triumph

The church is not just a community of the redeemed — it is the embassy of Christ's victory. In Ephesians 3:10, Paul writes that *"through the church, the manifold wisdom of God should be made known to the rulers and authorities in the heavenly realms."*

This is staggering. The church is God's trophy case; it is His demonstration to the unseen realm that His plan has worked. Every time the church gathers in unity, worships in the face of trial, forgives one another, or extends grace to the lost, it declares the wisdom and power of God.

Our unity shames division. Our joy shames despair. Our perseverance shames defeat. Our purity shames corruption. The Church, in all its frailty, becomes the stage upon which the victory of the cross is displayed to principalities and powers.

This is why the church matters in spiritual warfare. It's not just a support group for struggling believers — it is the training ground for Kingdom warriors. It is where faith is nurtured, Scripture is taught, wounds are healed, gifts are activated, and authority is practiced.

Satan's greatest strategy is not persecution — it is division. A fractured Church loses credibility and power. But a united, Spirit-filled, Word-saturated Church is unstoppable. Jesus said the gates of hell will not prevail against it (Matthew 16:18). That is not just a promise — it's a prophecy.

To be part of the Church is to be part of Christ's triumph. We don't attend Church — we are the Church. We carry the mission, the message, and the mantle of victory wherever we go. The Church is not weak — it is the fullness of Him who fills everything in every way.

How then shall I live?

Live as one who is already victorious. You are not fighting for identity or approval — you are fighting from it.

The victory of Christ is not something you must earn—it's something you receive and walk in. Remind yourself daily: the cross was enough.

Reject shame and accusation. Satan's primary weapon now is the lie. He will accuse you of sins already forgiven, failures already redeemed, and weaknesses already covered by grace. Resist him by clinging to the truth. You are not condemned—you are in Christ (Romans 8:1).

Walk in the authority of Christ. The same power that raised Jesus from the dead lives in you. That's not a metaphor—it's a miracle. Speak truth boldly. Pray with confidence. Bind what needs to be bound. Loose what needs to be loosed. Not in arrogance, but in alignment with Jesus.

Stay anchored in the Word. The sword of the Spirit is only effective if it is wielded. Know the Scriptures. Memorize them. Declare them. Let the Word of God be the loudest voice in your life. Lies cannot stand where truth is proclaimed.

Abide in prayer. Prayer is your supply line. It is the power cord of spiritual warfare. Do not wait for crisis—pray pre-emptively. Praise in advance. Intercede constantly. Listen attentively. The praying believer is a powerful force in the Kingdom.

Commit to the church. Do not fight alone. You were never meant to. Isolation is vulnerability. Community is strength. Serve the Church. Be discipled. Disciple others. Be accountable. Share your gifts. The victory of the cross is visible in the unity of the Church.

Advance the Kingdom. The best way to push back darkness is to turn on the light. Share the gospel. Love radically. Forgive quickly. Live generously. Speak life. Where the rule of Christ is established, the enemy loses ground.

Live with confidence, not complacency. The battle is real, but the outcome is sure. Do not be afraid of Satan—he is defeated. But do not be careless either—he is cunning. Stay awake. Stay armoured. Stay close to Jesus.

The cross was the great turning point in the cosmic war. It was the moment the tide turned forever. Christ triumphed — not only for Himself, but for us. And now we live in that triumph, not as spectators, but as participants.

The war is won. The tomb is empty. The King is risen. The Spirit is within. The Church is marching. And the enemy is in retreat. So, stand in the shadow of the cross. Walk in the light of the resurrection. Live in the authority of the ascension. And proclaim to every power and principality:

Jesus Christ is Lord.

11. RESISTING THE DEVIL

Understanding the call to resistance

The phrase *"deliver us from the evil one"* in the Lord's Prayer is more than a general plea for safety or protection. It is a deeply theological and spiritual petition for God to rescue us from the active presence and schemes of the evil one. Jesus taught His disciples to pray this way, not because they were paranoid or spiritually immature, but because He knew the reality of spiritual warfare that every believer would face.

The apostle James writes, *"Submit yourselves, then, to God. Resist the devil, and he will flee from you."* (James 4:7). The call to resist the devil is not optional for the Christian life—it is essential. Likewise, Peter warns, *"Be alert and of sober mind. Your enemy the devil prowls around like a roaring lion looking for someone to devour. Resist him, standing firm in the faith."* (1 Peter 5:8–9).

Both of these exhortations are anchored in a sober understanding of who Satan is and how he operates. They are not calls to fear, but to readiness. The call to resist is not about panic or obsession—it is about standing in the victory of Christ and refusing to surrender any ground.

To resist the devil is to take a stand against his lies, his temptations, and his influence in every area of life. It is to say, with your actions and your convictions, *"I will not partner with darkness."* It is an act of allegiance, of worship, and of warfare. It is spiritual defiance rooted in faith. But this resistance is not something we conjure up in our own strength. It flows from submission to God. James is clear: *"Submit yourselves, then, to God."* Without submission, resistance is totally futile. Without surrender to Christ's Lordship, we're vulnerable to every attack.

This is where many spiritual warfare teachings fall short. They emphasize authority without obedience, power without intimacy, warfare without worship. But Scripture always begins with surrender. We resist by abiding. We overcome by drawing near.

Recognizing the enemy's strategies

To resist the devil, we must recognize how he works. Scripture gives us a clear picture of his methods, and they have not changed. Though his tactics are adapted to culture and context, his core strategies remain the same: deception, temptation, accusation, intimidation, and distraction.

Deception is Satan's primary weapon. Jesus called him *"the father of lies"* (John 8:44). From the beginning, in the garden of Eden, he twisted God's word, distorted truth, and sowed doubt. He still does this today—especially among believers who are unfamiliar with the Scriptures. When we do not know God's Word, we are vulnerable to half-truths, false teachings, and worldly ideologies masked as wisdom.

Temptation is the lure toward sin, often by appealing to legitimate desires in illegitimate ways. Satan tempted our Lord Jesus in the wilderness not with grotesque evils, but with very plausible shortcuts. *"Turn these stones to bread." "Throw yourself down and prove your identity." "Bow down and gain the kingdoms of the world."* Temptation very often wears the mask of self-promotion, false comfort or convenience.

Accusation is the enemy's post-sin strategy. After luring us into compromise, he becomes the accuser, heaping shame, guilt, and despair on the believer. Revelation 12:10 calls him *"the accuser of our brothers and sisters."* His goal is to paralyze us with condemnation and drive a wedge between us and God's grace.

Intimidation is the tactic of fear. He wants us to feel powerless, overwhelmed, and isolated. He roars like a lion—not to devour immediately, but to scare prey into making a mistake. Fear makes us flee when we should stand. Fear makes us silent when we should speak.

Distraction is perhaps his most subtle weapon in the modern age. If he cannot deceive, tempt, accuse, or intimidate, he will settle for distraction. A busy, hurried, entertained, screen-addicted Christian is often too numb to notice spiritual attack. The devil doesn't need to possess us if he can simply preoccupy us.

Resisting the devil means resisting all of these strategies. It means identifying the lie and replacing it with truth; rejecting temptation and embracing holiness; silencing accusation with the blood of Christ; confronting fear with the promises of God; and trading distraction for devotion.

This requires spiritual discernment. We must be aware of what is happening beneath the surface. Not everything that feels natural is of God. Not every thought that passes through our mind is our own. Not every emotion is spiritually neutral. We are in a battle, and resistance begins with awareness.

Avoiding two dangerous extremes

As we consider spiritual warfare and resisting the devil, it's important to avoid two common and equally dangerous extremes: *denial* and *obsession*.

The first extreme is *denial* — acting as if the devil does not exist or has no relevance in the Christian life. Some believers and even whole denominations functionally ignore the spiritual realm. They view Satan as a metaphor or an outdated concept. This renders them spiritually naïve and unprepared.

C.S. Lewis warned about this in the preface to his classic book *The Screwtape Letters*: "*There are two equal and opposite errors into which our race can fall about the devils. One is to disbelieve in their existence. The other is to believe, and to feel an excessive and unhealthy interest in them.*"

This brings us to the second extreme: obsession. Some Christians become preoccupied with the devil and demonic activity. They see Satan behind every inconvenience and spiritualize every circumstance. This leads to fear, superstition, and unbiblical practices.

Both extremes are very harmful. Denial makes us vulnerable; obsession makes us anxious. The biblical path is one of sober-minded vigilance. We are called to be alert, not afraid. We are not to magnify the devil — we are to magnify Christ.

Jesus and the apostles never made the devil the centre of their message. They acknowledged his presence and authority, but always in the context of Christ's greater power. Their focus was the Kingdom of God, not the kingdom of darkness.

Healthy resistance is Christ-centred. It exalts His name, rests in His victory, and walks in His truth. We do not need to rebuke the devil every hour—but we must resist him when he encroaches. We do not chase demons, but we do stand firm in the Spirit. To resist the devil today is to walk faithfully in the light. It is to be unshaken by the storm because our foundation is secure. It is to know the battle is real, but the war is won.

Living alert in a distracted world

One of the most effective strategies of the enemy in today's world is distraction. We live in an age of endless noise, instant gratification, digital saturation, and attention fatigue. The enemy need not tempt us with obvious evil if he can simply keep us spiritually drowsy.

Paul exhorts the Thessalonians, *"So then, let us not be like others, who are asleep, but let us be awake and sober"* (1 Thessalonians 5:6). Similarly, Peter says, *"Be alert and of sober mind. Your enemy the devil prowls around like a roaring lion."* (1 Peter 5:8). To be sober-minded means to be spiritually attentive, emotionally grounded, and mentally disciplined. It means not being swept away by every trend, conspiracy, or crisis. It means cultivating a life of prayer, Scripture, fellowship, and intentional focus.

Living alert in a distracted world doesn't mean becoming a recluse or technophobe. It means reclaiming your attention as a form of spiritual warfare. It means choosing silence over noise, depth over shallowness, devotion over distraction.

Believers today must ruthlessly eliminate hurry, create space for communion with God, and guard their inner life. We cannot resist an enemy we do not notice. We cannot fight a battle we are too busy to recognize. Wakefulness is a spiritual weapon.

Embracing the authority of the believer

Another essential key to resisting the devil is embracing the authority given to us in Christ. Many Christians live in fear or defeat not because the enemy is too strong, but because they have forgotten their position. Jesus said, *"I have given you authority... to overcome all the power of the enemy; nothing will harm you"* (Luke 10:19). Paul declared that God *"raised us up with Christ and seated us with him in the heavenly realms."* (Ephesians 2:6).

This is not theoretical — it is positional. We are in Christ, and Christ is seated above all powers and principalities. Therefore, we resist not from earth upward, but from heaven downward. We speak, pray, and act from victory, not for victory. This authority is not a magic word or a spiritual formula. It is relational. It flows from intimacy with Jesus. The sons of Sceva in Acts 19 learned this the hard way: they tried to invoke Jesus' name without knowing Him, and the demons overpowered them.

Authority in Christ is exercised through alignment with Christ. It requires walking in the Spirit, obeying the Word, and staying submitted to the Father. When we do, our words carry weight, our prayers shift things, and our lives push back darkness. This does not mean every battle will be easy or every outcome will be immediate. But it does mean we fight from a place of security, not insecurity. We are not powerless victims — we are Spirit-empowered sons and daughters.

The Church has too often oscillated between arrogance and apathy. True authority is humble, confident, and anchored in the cross. When believers understand who they are and whose they are, the devil flees.

How then shall I live?

Live awake. Refuse to be lulled into spiritual sleep by busyness, entertainment, or complacency. Choose wakefulness. Cultivate a life of prayer and presence. Watch for the enemy — not in fear, but in faith. Pay attention to what's happening beneath the surface.

Live submitted. Start every day in surrender. Give God your thoughts, desires, habits, and plans. Resistance begins with submission. When you live under His authority, you walk in His power. Pride opens the door to attack; humility shuts it.

Live grounded. Know the Word of God. Stand firm in the truth. Let Scripture shape your convictions and calibrate your conscience. Don't let culture define your worldview — let Christ do that. When the lies come, answer with the truth.

Live connected. Resist isolation. Stay rooted in a good Christian community. Be honest, accountable, and known. Pray with others. Worship with others. Fight alongside others. The lone sheep is always the most vulnerable. The connected believer is covered.

Live clean. Close every door to sin, compromise, and darkness. Don't give the devil a foothold. Forgive quickly. Repent often. Walk in the light. Holiness is not about perfection — it's about protection. A clean heart is a strong defence.

Live confident. Don't shrink back in fear or shame. You are in Christ. You have His Spirit. You carry His authority. The same power that raised Jesus from the dead lives in you. Resist the devil — and he will flee.

Live focused. Eliminate distractions. Prioritize your spiritual disciplines. Give God your best attention. Read, meditate, and memorize Scripture. Speak it aloud. Pray it with boldness. Let your life be shaped by the eternal, not the urgent.

Live victorious. You are not under attack — you are on assignment. You're not just surviving — you're advancing. Don't just play defence — go on offense. Share the gospel. Love radically. Pray boldly. Wherever the light shines, the darkness must retreat. You were born into a battle, but you were born again into victory. Jesus has already won. The enemy is already defeated. And you, beloved child of God, have everything you need to stand. So live like it. Walk like it. Fight like it. **Resist the devil — and he will flee from you.**

12. FULLY EQUIPPED FOR BATTLE

Christ in you: the true armour

In Paul's letter to the Ephesians, he famously exhorts believers to *"put on the full armour of God"* so that they can stand against the devil's schemes (Ephesians 6:11). For generations, too many Christians have interpreted this command as a daily ritual—an act of spiritual clothing, often accompanied by prayers that mimic donning a helmet, a breastplate, a shield, and so on. While well-intentioned, such practices miss the deeper truth Paul was proclaiming. **The armour of God is not a metaphorical wardrobe we reach for in times of need—it is the very person of Jesus Christ, already present within us.**

This is not poetic exaggeration. It is the heart of the gospel. Paul was not offering a mystical practice; he was declaring a spiritual reality. Every element of the armour described in Ephesians 6 is a direct expression of Christ Himself: truth, righteousness, peace, faith, salvation, and the Word of God. These are not external garments we must earn or locate—they are the internal resources already gifted to us in Christ. When we are born again, we are not handed spiritual accessories; we are united with a Person. That Person is the victorious, risen Lord Jesus, who has already overcome the powers of darkness.

Paul's call to *"put on the armour"* is best understood as a call to *recognise* and *walk in* the reality of Christ within us. We are not spiritually naked one day and clothed the next depending on our performance. If Christ is in us, then His strength, His truth, and His righteousness are ours—not because we feel them, but because they are His, and He is ours.

This truth liberates the weary believer from the pressure of spiritual performance. So many have felt defeated before they even begin the day, convinced they forgot to *"put on the armour"* in the morning or say the right prayer. But our security does not hinge on our memory or our rituals—it rests on the unshakable presence of Christ within us.

The enemy's greatest tactic is not always overt attack, but subtle deception. If he can convince us that we're unprotected or exposed, then he can fill us with fear and self-doubt. But if we know who is in us — and what that means — we will not easily be moved.

The armour revealed in Christ

Let us consider the pieces of the armour in Ephesians 6 again as I close this book – but not as symbolic objects, but rather as manifestations of Christ Himself:

- *The belt of truth:* Jesus said, "I am the way and the truth and the life" (John 14:6). Truth is not a concept we acquire; it is a Person we receive. When Christ is in us, we are anchored in unchanging, eternal truth — even when lies swirl around us.

- *The breastplate of righteousness:* "This is his name by which he will be called: The Lord Our Righteous Saviour" (Jeremiah 23:6). Our protection is not our performance, but Christ's righteousness imputed to us. We don't earn this armour; we receive it.

- *Feet fitted with the readiness of the gospel of peace:* Christ Himself is our peace (Ephesians 2:14). Wherever we walk, we carry the presence of the Prince of Peace.

- *The Shield of Faith:* Jesus is the *"pioneer and perfecter of faith"* (Hebrews 12:2). Faith is not something we muster up; it is something that grows as we fix our eyes on Him.

- *The helmet of salvation:* Christ is our salvation. *"The Lord is my light and my salvation — whom shall I fear?"* (Psalm 27:1). Our minds are guarded when they are stayed on Him.

- *The sword of the Spirit:* Jesus is the living Word (John 1:1). The written Word is powerful because it reveals the Living One who defeated Satan with, *"It is written."*

When Paul tells us to take up the armour, he is not asking us to do something new each day — he is calling us to *remember who we are in Christ*, and to *stand* in that truth.

The entire letter to the Ephesians builds to this moment. Paul begins by declaring we are *"blessed with every spiritual blessing in Christ."* (1:3), and now he ends by telling us how to stand in that blessing, resisting the attacks of the enemy. The armour is not about acquiring power but about *abiding in presence.*

Standing, not striving

Three times in the space of four verses (Ephesians 6:11–14), Paul tells believers to *"stand."* Not fight. Not chase. Not strive. This is a posture of confidence, of settled identity, of immovable resolve. It implies that the ground has already been won. The battle is not for victory but *from* victory. Christ has already triumphed over the powers and principalities (Colossians 2:15), and now He calls His people to stand firm in what He has secured.

This does not mean spiritual warfare is passive. But it means the power behind our resistance is not our striving — it is our union with Christ. Standing is not inactivity; it is *spiritual alignment.* When we understand that Christ is our armour, we begin to see resistance not as something we struggle to maintain, but as something we *inherit and express.*

To stand in Christ is to silence the whispers of fear. It is to refuse the condemnation of the accuser. It is to hold ground in the face of temptation, not because we are strong, but because the One in us is stronger. And when we stumble — and we will — we do not fall out of the armour. We don't need to *"put it back on."* We simply turn again to the One who already holds us, already covers us, already lives within us. The real battle is for our awareness — our spiritual alertness to the truth of Christ in us.

The Spirit within: our ever-present strength

Alongside the indwelling Christ, the believer has another divine helper: the Holy Spirit. If the armour of God is the manifestation of Christ in us, then the power to live in that reality comes through the Spirit. Jesus said the Spirit would guide us into all truth, remind us of what He taught, and empower us to be His witnesses (John 14:26; Acts 1:8).

He is not an occasional visitor or a distant influence—He is a constant presence, a living Person who inhabits the lives of believers. The Holy Spirit is not a supplement to the Christian life—He *is* the Christian life. Without the Spirit, we cannot see clearly, discern truth, resist temptation, or walk in obedience. But with Him, every spiritual weapon becomes active, every fruit becomes possible, and every command becomes an invitation rather than a burden.

It is the Spirit who illuminates our union with Christ, who brings the armour to life within us. He convicts us of truth, strengthens us in weakness, and intercedes for us in our groanings. He is our Advocate, our Comforter, our Guide, and our Power. Spiritual warfare is not won by those who shout the loudest or strive the hardest, but by those who are most surrendered to the Spirit's leading.

When Paul says to *"pray in the Spirit on all occasions with all kinds of prayers"* (Ephesians 6:18), he is not prescribing a specific formula. He is inviting us into *continual communion* with the Spirit—an ongoing awareness of and dependence on God's presence. This is how we stand. This is how we resist. Not by gritting our teeth, but by walking in step with the Spirit (Galatians 5:25).

Living from victory, Not for victory

One of the enemy's most effective strategies is to reverse the gospel—to convince us that we must fight *for* what Christ has already given. This leads to exhaustion, striving, and spiritual burnout. But the truth of the gospel is that we do not fight *for* victory—we fight *from* it. We resist the enemy not to gain ground, but to hold what has already been won.

This is why Paul's emphasis in Ephesians 6 is not on chasing demons or breaking curses, but on *standing firm*. The battle has already been decided at the cross. Jesus disarmed the powers and authorities and made a public spectacle of them, triumphing over them (Colossians 2:15).

Satan is a defeated foe. He is still active, but his power is limited. His authority has been stripped, and his doom is certain. Yet he persists in accusing, deceiving, and intimidating. He aims to rob us of joy, confidence, and peace—not because he can defeat us, but because he can distract us. But when we live in the awareness of Christ's victory and the Spirit's presence, we walk in a settled authority. We speak truth to lies. We answer accusation with grace. We meet fear with faith. We do not run—we stand.

Victory in spiritual warfare is not measured by how much we chase the enemy, but by how deeply we abide in Christ. The fruit of the Spirit—love, joy, peace, patience, and the rest—are not signs of spiritual passivity, but evidence of spiritual strength. They are the fruit of someone who knows who they are, whose they are, and where they stand.

Warfare that looks like peace

Perhaps the greatest paradox of spiritual warfare is that it often looks like peace. Not the absence of conflict, but the presence of inner calm in the midst of it. It looks like forgiveness when you're wounded. Joy when life is hard. Truth when the world celebrates lies. It looks like praying for your enemies and blessing those who curse you. It looks like resting in the finished work of Christ while the enemy roars around you.

This is what confuses the kingdom of darkness—believers who are unshaken, not because they're trying harder, but because they're trusting deeper. Satan expects resistance, but not *peaceful* resistance. He expects shouting and striving—but not quiet confidence rooted in Christ. He expects ritual—but not intimacy. He expects fear—but not joy.

To live in Christ, clothed in His armour and filled with His Spirit, is to become an enigma to the enemy. You are no longer predictable. You are no longer able to be manipulated. You are dangerous—not because you wield human strength, but because you walk in divine authority. And that authority is not something you earn. It is not a badge for elite Christians. It is the inheritance of every child of God.

If you are in Christ, then you are clothed in Him. If you are clothed in Him, then you are fully equipped for battle. Even when you don't feel it. Even when you fail. Even when you forget. This is the truth that sets you free: You already have everything you need.

Awake, armed, and advancing

The Christian life is not a passive existence. Though the war has been won in Christ, we are still called to live as active participants in the unfolding drama of redemption. We are not spectators. We are not civilians. We are soldiers — not in the flesh, but in the Spirit. Our battlefield is the realm of the unseen: thoughts, emotions, worldviews, and temptations. The enemy may no longer have authority over us, but he will press every advantage if we live unaware or uncertain of who we are in Christ.

This is why Paul's call in Ephesians 6 is to *stand*, *resist*, and *pray*. These are the disciplines of the alert disciple. To stand is to remain rooted. To resist is to reject lies. To pray is to commune with the source of our strength. Together, these postures form the rhythm of victorious living.

Too many believers wait for a moment of crisis before they engage. But the truly equipped believer walks in a *daily awareness* of the spiritual battle — not paranoid, but prepared; not fearful, but faithful. We walk through this world as ambassadors of another Kingdom.

We carry the authority of Christ and the power of the Spirit. We don't just survive the enemy's attacks — we overturn them. We take ground by declaring truth, walking in love, and refusing to compromise.

And yet, all of this is only possible because of Christ in us and the Spirit upon us. The strength to stand is not generated by resolve but drawn from relationship. The more deeply we root ourselves in communion with God, the more immovable we become.

The power of a grounded identity

At the heart of all spiritual warfare is a question of identity. The serpent's first temptation to Eve began with a challenge to God's Word: *"Did God really say...?"* Jesus' first test in the wilderness began with a challenge to His identity: *"If you are the Son of God..."* And today, the enemy continues to ask: *Do you really know who you are? Are you really protected? Is God really with you?*

The armour of God is not about adding strength—it's about anchoring identity. When you know you are loved, chosen, and redeemed, the enemy loses his leverage. Accusation has no power over a forgiven heart. Temptation has no grip on a satisfied soul. Fear cannot dominate a mind that knows it is secure in Christ.

This is why truth matters. Not just doctrinal truth, but personal truth. You must know that Christ is your armour, that the Spirit is your helper, and that the Father calls you His own. These are not motivational slogans. They are spiritual realities that form the backbone of your resistance. The battle is rarely won in the dramatic moments—it is won in the quiet convictions, the settled confidence, the unwavering trust in the character of God.

You don't need more armour. You need more awareness. You don't need to chase after new anointings—you need to live in the fullness of the One who already lives in you.

How then shall I live?

You are not entering a battle hoping for victory—you are standing in victory, resisting an already-defeated foe. So let's ask on last time, how should you live?

- Live *alert*, knowing there is an enemy who schemes—but do not fear him.
- Live *rooted*, standing firm in the truth that Christ is your armour.

- Live *empowered*, drawing daily strength from the Holy Spirit who lives within you.

- Live *anchored*, holding fast to your identity in Christ no matter what storms may come.

- Live *prayerfully*, in communion with the God who fights for you and through you.

- Live *peacefully*, knowing the war is already won, and your future is secure.

- Live *boldly*, not because you are strong, but because Christ in you is.

You are already dressed for battle. You are already equipped. You are already victorious. So stand in the power of His might.

Stand with the belt of truth buckled around your waist—not because you put it there, but because Christ is the Truth and He lives in you.

Stand with the breastplate of righteousness guarding your heart—not your own righteousness, but the perfect covering of Christ.

Stand with your feet planted in the peace of the gospel, ready to walk wherever He leads.

Hold the shield of faith, not conjured up in your effort, but gifted to you by grace.

Wear the helmet of salvation, renewing your mind with the unshakable truth of who you are.

Wield the sword of the Spirit, the Word that speaks life into darkness.

And above all, *pray*. Not as a last resort, but as a first instinct. Not in desperation, but in confidence. Pray with all kinds of prayers and requests, not to awaken a distant God, but to align with the God who is already with you.

This is your inheritance. This is your authority. This is your armour. Now, walk in it.

www.ingramcontent.com/pod-product-compliance
Lightning Source LLC
Chambersburg PA
CBHW071232020426
42333CB00015B/1432